HISTORY AS MYTH
The Import for Contemporary Theology

HISTORY AS MYTH
The Import for Contemporary Theology

W. Taylor Stevenson

THE SEABURY PRESS · NEW YORK

TO MY MOTHER AND FATHER
Courage, discipline, hope

Contents

HISTORY AS MYTH
The Import for Contemporary Theology

Introduction

*Beneath the star of the promise
of God it becomes possible to
experience reality as "history."*
Jürgen Moltmann, THEOLOGY OF HOPE

*For King Midas, legend says,
everything he touched turned to gold.
For modern man everything, the whole
of reality, turns to history.*
Gerhard Ebeling, WORD AND FAITH

During the past two centuries, history has become increasingly the preoccupation of the Church, until today it is *the* fateful question for the Christian community. This development is quite appropriate, since during the same period it has become increasingly clearer within Western civilization as a whole that the understanding of the historical nature of reality is *the* distinguishing characteristic of our time. It is this that sets us apart not only from other civilizations but also, to a significant degree, from our own earlier understanding of ourselves and our world. It is widely stated, and very plausibly, of course, that the natural sciences and technology are the distinguishing marks of our civilization. Science and technology, on the one hand, and the modern historical consciousness, on the other hand, have important similari-

1

ties: a strict attentiveness to the world around; a keen sense
of man's responsibility for this world; an awareness of the
significance of the evolutionary process, whether this be
that of nature or of history; and so on. Moreover, as a
result of the work of Pierre Teilhard de Chardin, Leslie Dewart, Owen Barfield, and others, we are just beginning to
see that these two types of evolution are related. Nevertheless, as the following pages will make clear, we believe that
our sense of history is the more fundamental characteristic
of our civilization, supplying the incredible dynamic and
the high sense of creativity and purposefulness of human
life not only to the natural sciences but also to our civilization as a whole.

The development of this modern historical consciousness,
in which the cherished authorities, traditions, and interpretative schemata of past centuries were relentlessly and successfully challenged, has been aptly characterized by Van A.
Harvey as an "almost Promethean will-to-truth." [1] Before
the middle of the eighteenth century, such men as Giambattista Vico had decided that man himself, in the context of
the historical process, is the creator of his own world. Once
this decision started to gain acceptance, it was only a matter
of time before the logic of this position made it clear that
no area is exempt from the searching gaze of the historian.
Certainly the Scripture and traditions of the Church, which
were so profoundly a part of the civilization in which the
modern historical consciousness developed, were not exempt. It is to the permanent credit of nineteenth-century
liberalism that it brought history's "Promethean will-to-
truth" right into the Church in order to see what it was that
man had created there in terms of Scripture and tradition.

Neither the Church nor our civilization generally has yet
fully come to terms with the modern, self-conscious perception of the historical nature of reality, which emerged in
the eighteenth century. Consequently, and without retracting our judgment that the historical perception of the world

is *the* characteristic of our civilization, we could agree with Mircea Eliade that the understanding of man as a historical being "has not yet made a *definitive* conquest of contemporary thought." [2] (Nor is it likely that there will ever be a *definitive* conquest here.) There is, in spite of the dominant influence of history, a profound ambiguity in the attitude of our civilization toward history. Out of this ambiguity, there arise the "various recent orientations that tend to reconfer value upon the myth of cyclical periodicity," and which are a revolt against the terror of historical time in which man is—or appears to be—the creator and master of his world.[3] Certainly Toynbee's philosophy of history, with its emphasis upon the cycles of civilizations, is one prominent example of this revolt; and perhaps the work of T. S. Eliot and James Joyce, which Eliade sees as being "saturated with nostalgia for the myth of eternal repetition . . . [and] the abolition of time," [4] are other examples. History is tolerable, Eliade maintains, only when it is understood as having its guaranty and source in God.[5] Our civilization as a whole has not yet understood it in that way.

In its own way, the Christian faith also has not yet experienced the definitive victory of history in its own language and thought. The struggle, which earlier took the form of the controversy surrounding biblical criticism, has now found its focus in the whole issue of secularity. Within the context of the Christian faith, the terror of history is the terror of the radically historical, or "secular," understanding of the gospel. We say "radically historical" or "secular" because we believe that at its best the "secular" understanding of the gospel is, and is expressed more adequately in terms of, a radically historical understanding of the gospel.[6] That this approach to the gospel is "terrifying" is shown by the hue and cry raised by the death-of-God theology. (Admittedly, the terror was compounded by the "terror" of the coming together of an embryonic theological program with the media of mass communication!) When the po-

lemics and counterpolemics of the death-of-God theology
have died away, however, the fundamental problem to
which that movement pointed will remain and must be dealt
with. This problem, as Gordon Kaufman has pointed out, is
much deeper than that presented by the legends and the
sometimes elaborate and fantastic mythological imagery
that we encounter in the Scripture and traditions of the
Church. Rather, "the problem is whether there is *any significant reality at all* 'above' or 'beyond' or 'below' the world
which we know in our experience, or whether life is to be
understood simply in this-worldly, i.e., secular, terms." [7] If
the answer is that there is no other reality than historical
reality, and if historical reality is understood in the usual
way as being *only* that which man has created, then we are
indeed presented with the heady but terrifying prospect of
a universe grounded in man alone. We know too much
about ourselves not to be terrified by this prospect! If it is
decided that *this* is what is meant by a historical understanding of the gospel or of reality, then we may look forward
with confidence to a headlong rush by our civilization back
into some form of the myth of the eternal return.

In the recent past, and still to some extent today, we have
sought to protect ourselves from the terror of history by
making what has seemed to many to be a legitimate distinction between "ordinary" history (*Historie*) and the "salvation history" (*Heilsgeschichte*) in which God manifests
himself and his will for our world. This distinction, as we
shall see in our discussion of the theology of Rudolf Bultmann, permits him to quote with approval such statements
as: "The advent of Christ is an event in the realm of eternity
which is incommensurable with historical time." [8] This positing of a reality which is "above" or "in addition to" history serves very effectively, if it is accepted, to protect one
from the terror of history. However, this dichotomy between
history and salvation history has at least three serious consequences: it represents a step backward in the long struggle

to bring the Christian faith into the realm of history; it serves to fragment our world by making a fundamental distinction between ordinary history and that special history upon which our salvation is dependent; and it appears to leave unsatisfied those who raise the question as to just what that reality is which supposedly lies beyond ordinary history. For these and related reasons we will argue that the distinction between history and salvation history is more misleading than helpful, and therefore should be abandoned.

We will attempt to show that the way out of the impasse which we have outlined here is by way of a reappropriation of the meaning of the term "history." The meaning of this term has always been a matter of controversy in the modern period, beginning with the first systematic formulation of the modern historical consciousness in the work of Giambattista Vico (1668–1744), and principally in his *New Science* (1725). The reigning Cartesian philosophy in Vico's day had proclaimed the "clear and distinct idea" to be *the* criterion of all knowledge, including the knowledge gained through history. Vico, while admitting the appropriateness of Descartes's criterion for mathematics and the natural sciences, revolted against conceiving of history in these terms. This struggle has continued to the present day. Vico argued that the "clear and distinct idea" is inappropriate to history. History, far from being primarily concerned with "objective facts" (which are the historical equivalent of clear and distinct ideas) is by its very nature involved in the complexities and ambiguities of language, and in the difficulties of the interpretation of the language of the past to the present. With amazing incisiveness, Vico saw in the early eighteenth century this intimate relationship between language and history. That which constitutes a historical event cannot be dissociated from the linguistic description of that event. Vico's perception of the linguistic nature of history was ignored, however, and has only been taken up in a serious way relatively recently: earlier by Martin Buber in his pioneering work *I and Thou,* and then more recently and more explicitly by Martin Heidegger, by those associated with the "new hermeneutic," and by many others.

It is the first purpose of this study to examine certain aspects of the relationship between history, myth, and Christian theology; and second, in the course of our own discussion, to examine a number of representative expressions of modern and contemporary thought about history, and especially as it pertains to our understanding of the Christian faith. Our approach is necessarily very selective, and our case for the validity of this selective approach will have to rest upon the execution and conclusions of our investigation. In the course of our investigation we will contend that history is basically a mythic way of perceiving the world. Those who subscribe to the myth of history affirm that reality is historical in nature. The myth of history shares in what we take to be the formal characteristics of all myths. First, it gives to the community of those who participate in it their "true story" about man, nature, and the divine. Second, it is based upon certain originating events which are not demonstrably true in terms of other, more fundamental categories, but which call for decision on the part of those who accept them. Third, it arises with its own peculiar set of linguistic images, and there is no closer approach to reality than that which is afforded through these images. Narrowing our gaze specifically to the myth of history for a moment, the "true story" of reality is that man, nature, and God are historical in nature; the originating events are certain original *relational* events recorded in Scripture, and supremely the Incarnation; and the linguistic images which enable us to apprehend reality are those found in the language of history and, more fundamentally, in the language pertaining to the original relational event.

We believe we will be able to show that this approach to history, in addition to being faithful to biblical and classical Christian faith in all its fullness and uniqueness, carries with it the following advantages. First, it enables us to see that the "objective historical facts," which have loomed so large in recent discussion, are secondary abstractions derived from and dependent upon the mythical perception of reality as historical. Second, it possesses, because of its particular emphasis upon language, the potentiality for re-sensitizing us to the power and mystery of the word of man and the word of God, and their interrelationship. (The liturgical implications of this could be especially important for the life of the Church.) Third, because of man's integral part in the historical process, our approach enables us to see more clearly the exalted view of man implicit in the Incarnation. Whereas myths of the eternal return speak of man's "original participation" in the divine, marked by immediacy and passivity, the myth of history speaks of man's "final participation" in the divine, marked by our active and creative participation in the divine plan.[9] Fourth, through its radical emphasis upon the givenness and per-vasiveness of the original relational event and the myth of history which arises with it, our approach places an emphasis upon grace that is badly needed in the contemporary theological situation.[10] Fifth, arising out of its emphasis upon the word of God and grace, as well as the related evo-lutionary dimension of history, our approach gives us a base for engaging constructively in dialogue with the theology of such men as Pierre Teilhard de Chardin, as well as the more general contemporary reopening of discussion con-cerning the doctrine of creation. Sixth, growing out of the emphasis upon a view of reality which is both *community held and mythic,* our approach enables us to deal creatively with the closely interrelated problems of rationalism, in-dividualism, and subjectivism. Finally, because eschatology is intrinsic to the myth of history, our approach takes its place as a part of the renewed awareness of the eschatologi-cal dimension of the Christian faith which is being mani-fested across the entire face of contemporary theological discussion, and most emphatically in the "theology of hope" associated with Jürgen Moltmann. Moltmann affirms: "The eschatological is not one element *of* Christianity, but it is the medium of Christian faith as such, the key in which everything in it is set. . . ." [11] We agree; but we believe that the claim which Moltmann makes for "eschatology" can be made with even greater justice for the more inclusive concept of the "myth of history."

We now turn to our study to see if the claims made in this introduction can be validated.

1

History as a Form of Myth

At every level of contemporary thinking and action we find two outstanding characteristics. The first of these is the great respect accorded to the scientific method. The astoundingly successful use of this method both in basic scientific research and in its application to the problems of technology has affected every dimension of our lives. We cannot entirely foresee, as yet, where this whole development will eventually lead us.

This overwhelming impact of science and technology obscures to some extent the second outstanding characteristic of our contemporary approach to the world. This is our commitment to thinking historically. Indeed, we commonly assume that it is possible to think only in historical terms, that is, in terms of "facts" or "events," which give us the basis of all our knowledge, of historical origins and development, of the historically conditioned and hence tentative nature of our thinking, and so on.

If any cultural consensus is possible in our time, its chief and perhaps only components would be the importance of scientific methodology and the necessity of historical thinking. This is our vision of the world. This is not to say that other elements are not present in our view of the world; and specifically, the recrudescence of ahistorical elements in our culture, such as have been pointed out by Mircea Eliade and

9

others, cannot be ignored.¹ Nevertheless, the natural sciences
and history are still the major elements informing our contemporary vision of the world. Like all civilizations, we
instinctively claim a special status for this vision with its
characteristic mode of thinking and acting, a claim which
arises out of our conception of it as being self-evidently
right, the model for all correct thinking. Unlike other civilizations, however, our historical sense checks us; we know
that we cannot claim that our vision of the world is self-
evidently true. Neither scientific nor historical thinking is
"natural" in the sense of being a necessary mode of thinking
of the enlightened man.

We are led to ask, therefore, about the origin of our peculiar view of the world. It will be seen as we proceed that the
two facets of this view, scientific methodology and historical
thinking, are interrelated. It is, however, the origin of the
latter of these two which must be our particular concern
here if we are to go on to discuss the problem of history in
recent theology; for "the nature of [things] is nothing but
their coming into being (*nascimento*) at certain times and in
certain fashions." ² Therefore it will be our purpose in this
chapter to discuss the origin, and hence the nature, of
historical thinking in its most essential aspects. This will
involve stating our basic orientation to the phenomenon of
history, and the definition of several fundamental terms.

At several points in our discussion, the exodus of Israel
from Egypt, the Incarnation, and the Resurrection will be
either implicitly or explicitly in view. This does not mean,
however, that we are primarily interested in "holy history"
or a "theology of history," as these are usually understood.
Nor are we particularly interested in the speculative philosophy of history such as has been offered by Augustine,
Hegel, Marx, Toynbee and others, and which claims to be
able to plot the course of past and future history in terms
of some overarching scheme. Our concern, rather, is simply
with history as that term is commonly used, and as it under-

lies the multitudinous particular interpretations of specific events and of history as a whole. We will be asking: What does it mean to see human experience as being basically historical in nature? The discussion, and the definition at which we will eventually arrive, will indeed say that history, or the historical interpretation of reality, cannot be understood apart from the biblical witness to the acts of God found in the Old and New Testaments. Therefore, if you wish, we might be said to be defining history in some sense as "holy history." If one chooses this formulation of the matter, however, it must be emphasized that *all* history is holy history; the history of Marxism, as much as biblical or church history. For ourselves, we will avoid the term "holy history" as far as possible, because it misleadingly implies that there are somehow two kinds of phenomena: holy events, or history; and, presumably, unholy events, or history.

Relatively little attention has been given to this problem of the origin and nature of historical consciousness as such. This stands in contrast to the large amount of work which has been done, first, in the field of speculative philosophy of history (Hegel, Marx, Spengler, Toynbee, etc.) and, second, in regard to specific problems within historical thinking, such as historical causation and necessity.[3] It is, nevertheless, beyond the scope of this book to make a detailed survey and individual critique of even the relatively limited possibilities that have been advanced as to the nature of historical consciousness. However, a few general remarks in this area will be useful before we go on to state our own position.

THREE COMMON ATTITUDES TOWARD HISTORY

In general terms, what are the possibilities which are open to us for understanding the historical consciousness that is so much a part of our world? To begin with, we

should discuss briefly that approach to history which exam-
ines its nature in order to be able to dismiss it in favor of
some supposedly more ultimate level of understanding, for
example, that of economics or psychology. In regard to this
possibility we need to say two things. First, and most important, the attempts to reduce the complexity of historical
phenomena to a relatively restricted set of such phenomena
are of very limited value because, as the discussion which
will follow should make clear, those who take such an approach are still working in terms of a view of reality that is
basically historical in nature. For example, to say that history may be understood in terms of one limited portion of
history, such as that described by Marxian economics, does
not go far toward explaining why we see the world as being
historical in nature in the first place. Second, insofar as
what we know as history is genuinely dissolved into the
ahistorical categories of psychology or Indian philosophy,
for example, then our consciousness of the world as being
historical in nature has not been explained or even directly
criticized; rather, it has been renounced in favor of another
world-view, and one which calls for judgment and decision
as to its own validity.

A second and much commoner attitude toward the historical view of reality is to accept it simply and unreflec-
tively, and to leave the matter there. This attitude, so
understandable because our awareness of history is literally
given to us with our very language, may be supported in
various ways. Thus it may be said, for example, that historical thinking is the self-evidently correct and universal approach to experience for anyone who has moved beyond
ignorance and superstition. Or again, in a slightly more
critical spirit, it may be admitted that, while presumably
historical thinking has an origin which affects its character,
and while knowledge of this origin might be instructive as
to the theoretical basis of such thinking, nevertheless speculation about such matters is uninteresting or unimportant

or impossible—or all three. This attitude wins hands-down, of course, in our pragmatic society, which is oriented so strongly to a constant escalation of both production and consumption. Speculation gets in the way of production and consumption! In this situation, origins and ends (always so closely related) are uncritically accepted from "somewhere else," or as having "gradually evolved." Real life, according to this view, is lived between origins and ends, in the realm of means; which is to say, in the realm of production and consumption. This point of view, when applied to the discipline of history, tells us to attend to the production and consumption of research in regard to specific historical problems. Such thinking has both the strengths and the weaknesses of all strictly pragmatic orientations to experience.[4]

A third possible attitude toward history is to assert that a hard core of historical fact exists independently of the articulation and interpretation of the historian. This is the position which so competent a historian as Barbara Tuchman believes she holds.[5] Of course, neither Miss Tuchman nor anybody else actually understands or writes history on this basis; although occasionally one does encounter an approximation to this approach in those incredibly tedious books which seem to have been produced through the selective arrangement of a large number of laboriously prepared file cards.

If one were to accept this position seriously, however, how would the investigation of history proceed? Presumably one would proceed through the selection and arrangement of the given units of historical reality, the so-called brute facts of history. To use R. G. Collingwood's phrase, this would be a "scissors-and-paste" operation. Then, to this selective arrangement of data, which might or might not be admitted to be in itself an interpretation, would be added an interpretation.

A great many things might be said about this understand-

ing of history; but, for our purposes, it is sufficient to make
the following observations. The belief that a hard core of historical fact exists independently of the interpretation of the
historian is a fallacy that has persistently confused historical
thought throughout the modern period. As is usually the case
with ideas that are hard to eradicate, however, the persist-
ence of this idea is due in part to its pointing to some continuing and valid aspect of human experience. In this case,
what is being pointed to is the "continuing round" of human
activity. This is part of the givenness of all human experience; as is witnessed by the ancient and universal practice of
making chronicles, especially of the "continuing round" of
those who exercise some form of authority or power. May
such chronicles, bare lists of names and dates and events,
be said to exist apart from the interpretation of the historian?
Yes, but not as historical "facts." Properly speaking, they
are not historical facts at all. Everything depends upon how
one sees the chronicle, that is, everything depends upon the
imagination of the beholder. Is the record of the "continuing
round" counted as illusion, as is the case from the perspective of Hinayana Buddhism? If so, there is no possibility of
the chronicle being perceived as historical in nature. Or, as
has been the case in the West, is the chronicle looked upon
as recorded fragments of a meaningful process? If so, then
reality is seen as historical, and the chronicle may come to
play an essential but limited part in exploring historical
reality.

It would be misleading, however, if, having granted this
very limited validity to the concern for "objective facts," we
were to say no more. The preoccupation with objective facts
as some kind of core reality is not a universal, but a peculiarly Western, phenomenon. This preoccupation is the
result of a view of the world, owing much to Descartes,
which, first, sees the individual's internal world of the mind
as being separate and independent from the external world
of the body; and, second, conceives of the individual's ap-

prehension of the external world as a private, nonverbal *seeing* of that which is clear and distinct—the "objective fact." In this orientation to experience, "The entire universe consists essentially or basically of objects—things. Persons and the consciousness they exhibit are unaccountable intrusions, foreign to objective reality, which is voiceless and normally passive." [6]

This understanding of experience, as Vico was already pointing out in the eighteenth century, renders historical consciousness and inquiry impossible; for history is verbal, social, and does not characteristically deal with clear and distinct ideas.[7] Consequently, while Miss Tuchman and others may *believe* that objective historical facts exist independently of the historian, this is an intellectualization which really has no significant relation to their consciousness of history and their practice as historians. The "facts" of history are actually, as our subsequent discussion will make clear, secondary abstractions derived from the fullness of historical consciousness and practice, the nature of which we now wish to begin to describe.

MYTH AND HISTORY

The three attitudes toward history which we have described, while by no means exhaustive, do cover much of the contemporary discussion in this area. It is against this background that we wish to introduce a fourth major possibility. This approach to history, which as we shall see finds expression in a variety of ways in various contemporary authors, is the one that we wish to explore in the remainder of this book. At the risk of being misunderstood here, and of being slightly repetitious later, we wish at this point to describe this view of history very concisely. We would attempt to state it in the following way. History is a way of perceiving and ordering the totality of human experience in which ultimate or sacral meaning is understood to be present in empirical and transitory phenomena. Moreover, the historical process is seen to be driving forward in hope to an ever greater realization of meaning. The historical understanding of reality is oriénted primarily toward those phenomena which are the creation of man, and above all toward the phenomenon of man himself; but it also encompasses every area of experience, including our experience of nature. Consequently, history is both evolutionary and humanistic—when these terms are correctly, i.e., historically, understood.

Like every other view of reality, history is productive of a comprehensive intellectual and social organization of the world, although its truth cannot be argued conclusively. Thus, for example, there can be no conclusive demonstration of the rightness or superiority of the historical understanding of experience over the ultimately ahistorical understanding of experience subscribed to by the Buddhist. Nevertheless, those who affirm that reality is historical in nature (and in regard to this fundamental point, this would include all of those who assume the latter two of the three attitudes which we have outlined above) claim that this is the "true story" of how the world is and is to be perceived. It is just these characteristics which we take to be the essential aspects of any myth: that it is the true story about the sacral power which invests man and the world; and, that it enables us to perceive and organize all realms of our experience. It is history, we would argue, which enables us to do this in our civilization; and consequently we would maintain that history is our myth. The insistence of most persons that history is no myth, that is, no "false story," but the *objective* (true!) account of our experience of the world, demonstrates the continuing vitality of the myth of the historical nature of reality.

The work of Mircea Eliade on myth represents a widespread consensus as to meaning of myth, and we believe that our contention that history is a mythic perception of reality is compatible with this consensus. In *Myth and*

Reality, Eliade gives five characteristic qualities of myth.[8]
First, myth "constitutes the History of the acts of the Supernaturals." [9] The myth of history, we would affirm, speaks
of the "history of the Supernaturals" by speaking of the
history of man. In history, man has become "Supernatural"
—the creator and ruler of the world. This divinization of
man comes to pass in the myth of history for good reasons,
reasons which we will explore in the following chapters.
Second, says Eliade, the story or history recounted in any
myth is "absolutely *true* (because it is concerned with realities) and *sacred* (because it is the work of the Supernaturals)." [10] If it is granted that men are the "Supernaturals,"
then this second characteristic quality of myth applies
clearly to the myth of history. Our unreserved commitment
to the validity of history and the importance of historical
truth witnesses to this situation. No more damning criticism
can be made of anyone than that of having falsified history,
i.e., of having tampered with the "true" and the "sacred."
Third, according to Eliade, "myth is always related to a
'creation,' it tells how something came into existence. . . .
this is why myths constitute the paradigms for all significant
human acts." [11] History, the "true" story of what has come
to pass, is the myth which supplies the dominant paradigm
for our civilization. Fourth, "by knowing the myth one knows
the 'origin' of things and hence can control and manipulate
them at will." [12] Here it only needs to be added that the
manipulation and control exercised through any myth never
violates the myth itself. Hence, the control which we exercise over events though the myth of history does not give
us control over the myth itself; or, the control proceeds from
the myth, and not vice versa, as many people strangely sup-
pose. The importance of this quality of the myth of history
will become clearer as we proceed. Fifth, concludes Eliade,
and this is clearly applicable to history, "one 'lives' the myth,
in the sense that one is seized by the sacred, exalting power
of the events recollected or re-enacted." [13]
   We believe that what is often called "historical con-

sciousness" conforms essentially to what Eliade calls "myth," and consequently we may assert that history is a mythic way of viewing reality. Moreover, we believe that the *consistent* recognition that this is so will clarify our understanding of history and of ourselves. If this is so, then it follows naturally that our understanding of the Christian faith will also be clarified.

THE ORIGIN OF THE MYTH OF HISTORY

Now that we have given preliminary definitions of history, myth, and the myth of history, we are in a position to discuss the origin of the myth of history. As we have already stated, our position is that historical consciousness originates in the experience described in the Old and New Testaments. This position is widely held, although some (for example, most of those described above in the section "Three Common Attitudes toward History") would dissent from our position. Our task at this point is to describe concisely the most significant characteristics of biblical experience which are *also* characteristics of our modern historical consciousness. (We believe that this similarity is sufficiently evident that we will not have to insist upon it repetitiously at each step in our argument.) It is not our intention here to say that the experience of Israel and later the Church *eventually* gave rise to our historical consciousness; but, rather, that biblical experience *is* historical experience. The myth of history informs them both. (The eventual *modification* of the myth of history, for example, the increasing self-consciousness about history, is the subject of succeeding chapters.) We believe, and we hope our discussion will show, that the correspondence between biblical and historical experience is so clear that the burden of proof is placed upon those who would deny that myth of history originates in biblical experience.

The inner dynamic of both biblical experience and historical experience is founded upon the same reality: the covenant between God and man. Everything proceeds from the covenant event. The elements within the covenant event which are most significant, at least for our purposes, are: (1) the giving and receiving of a promise, and the ongoing and continually renewed expectation of the fulfillment of that promise; (2) the radical and continuing involvement of God in the historical process; (3) the constituting of certain persons, places, and times as of eternal significance for God and man; and (4) the radical responsibility of man for the historical process. Let us look at each of these four elements in turn.

Promise and Fulfillment. As a result of the past generation of biblical scholarship, we have come to see the theme of promise and fulfillment as absolutely fundamental to biblical experience.[14] In discussions of this theme, our attention is often directed to such passages as Deuteronomy 7:8ff.:

. . . it is because the Lord loves you, and is keeping the oath which he swore to your fathers, that the Lord has brought you out with a mighty hand, and redeemed you from the house of bondage, from the hand of Pharaoh king of Egypt. Know therefore that the Lord your God is God, the faithful God who keeps covenant and steadfast love with those who love him and keep his commandments, to a thousand generations (RSV).

The covenant promise is given to Israel in the exodus. This, however, is only the beginning of the relationship; a fact which is seen most clearly in the promise of Yahweh which includes the promise to Israel of a land which is not yet theirs. It is only as Yahweh and Israel go forward together into Canaan to take the land that Israel comes to know that Yahweh is faithful, and to know the specific ways in which this faithfulness manifests itself. Like all significant relationships, this one is marked by tension, ambiguity and surprise. Not only within the exodus, but also in the successive prophetic movements and then in the messianic expectation, everything moves within the tension between Yahweh's promise and the fulfillment of that promise. This tension gives rise to the questioning of the promise: How shall we account for the delay in the fulfillment of the promise? When and how will this further fulfillment come? Moreover, the fulfillments which do come—the conquest of Canaan, deliverance from the enemy—are partial. Each fulfillment gives rise to a further promise.

How shall we read the ambiguous signs of the time (Isa. 4:2–6; 10:24–27; Jer. 14:16ff.; Zech. 10:6–12)? This questioning and anxiety in turn leads Israel into a thankless rebelliousness against Yahweh, further compounding the tension and anxiety (II Kings 17:7ff.; Pss. 78; 106). Nevertheless, although Israel is faithless, Yahweh is not. In spite of all of Israel's transgressions, Yahweh "will give her vineyards, and make the Valley of Achor a door of hope. And there she shall answer as in the days of her youth, as at the time when she came out of the land of Egypt" (Hos. 2:15). In the circumstances, each successive fulfillment of the promise can be experienced only as grace and as surprise. "Thus in Israel all history is a movement between promise and fulfillment. What God promises he fulfills, and, because the fulfillment is only partial, it contains within it an unfulfilled promise that points forward to a new fulfillment." [15]

This is the understanding of experience which the exodus brings about; an understanding which bears all of the essential characteristics of what we have come to call the "historical understanding of reality." First and foremost this is so because to live out of the exodus event is, as in all historical experience, to be oriented toward the future and the fulfillment which it will bring. The cry from Moses through the prophets to Jesus and beyond is always: "Let thy kingdom come!" This, of course, is in no sense to renounce the past; it is from the past that the promises come. The attitude toward the past is one of gratitude and thanksgiving; but the past is never an end in itself, and the desire to return to a Golden Age is, at best, a peripheral motif in biblical experience. For biblical-historical experience, the Golden Age is in the future; the promises can only be progressively understood in the light of their successive fulfillments. The myth of history, whether in its biblical or contemporary manifestation, is marked by a radical orientation toward the future in which the significance of the totality of human experience is seen as evolving in ever new ways.

God and History. Second, and inseparable from what we have just said, the promises are known to be God's promises, and the successive fulfillments in the course of history are understood to have been effected by God. There can be no question of how God "gets into history," for history is *of God*. History, for this reason, is expressive of sacral meaning. The realm of history is the realm of God's rule. God is committed to history. This is not to be committed to something which is strange to him; but, rather, he is committed to that which he has himself created through the promises of the covenant event and through the ongoing fulfillments of that event. This process of fulfillment is a most inclusive one, and not restricted simply to the social and political movements of history. Thus, James Barr wishes to leave room for the "direct verbal communication" between God and man, and believes that the stress upon history is inimical to such communication.[16] This is not necessarily so, as we shall see; it only being necessary to insist that if there is "direct verbal communication" between God and man, then it takes place within the myth of history.

It is because history is of the one God of the exodus, and because it drives toward the fulfillment which is in accordance with his will, that history (whether biblical or "secular") is understood to have a unity. Certainly there is little about the events of history which would indicate to anyone who does not participate in the myth of history that

there is a unity to history. Yet, the myth of history affirms
the unity of history to be "true." Thus, history is not irra-
tional, controlled by fate, under the "principalities and powers," or split by any irremedial dualism; rather, it is, poten-
tially at least, a coherent, meaningful whole. The impetus,
first in Judaism and then more fully in Christianity, toward
universal history is also an expression of this unity. (There
is a moral dualism of good and evil in history, but the
overcoming of this provisional dualism is witnessed to in
the drive toward the "Kingdom of God," the "classless society," "greater understanding," etc.) The unity of history
is the presupposition, part of the true story, of history. History is of God, and God is one.

It must be admitted, of course, that the one clear point
of divergence between the biblical and contemporary expressions of the myth of history is that in the latter form
there is characteristically no admission that history is of
God. The discussion of the complex reasons why this is so
will recur in the following chapters; but, if we had to
point to only one reason for this situation, it would be to
the not entirely innocent misunderstanding (by both the
Church and the so-called secular historians) of history in
terms of individually perceived, highly defined, and distinct
"facts." It is our contention that the understanding that history is mythic in nature points a way out of this misunderstanding.

Events: Persons, Places and Times. Because the covenant
is given through an event, the exodus, and because this
event involved what was said and done by specific persons,
at specific places and times, the exodus event thereby gives
"event" a very high significance. Moreover, because of the
tension between received promise and anticipated fulfillment, not only the original event, but also the events between promise and fulfillment are invested with great significance. Israel is anxious about and attentive toward
events, because in them the will of Yahweh is unfolded;

within the context of events the people Israel come to know
the God with whom they have to do, and who determines
who they are. Because events have this function, they are
loved; and because they are loved, they can be adequately
known.

It follows from this revolutionary attitude toward the
world (and not vice versa), that if the concrete events of
time and place are integral to the rule of God, then the
created order can only be accepted in thanksgiving as the
good creation (Gen. 1:31). The human and natural creation not only participates in the rule of God, but also is
instrumental to it. Here the earth can only be the blessed
earth. Consequently, "the escape from the created work
into bodiless spirit, into mind, is forbidden. God wills to
look upon his work, to love it, to call it good and preserve
it." [17] It is because of this that the Israelite, and later the
Christian, "hope remained loyal to this earth." [18] This vision
of the world, so much a part of our historical view of reality,
has affected the attitudes and actions of Western civilization
to a degree of which we are only now becoming fully aware.

Man and History. Another dimension of the tension, ambiguity, and resultant anxiety created by the exodus event is
man's sense of his responsibility for the fulfillment of the
promises of the covenant. Yahweh chose Israel, but Israel
also chose Yahweh; and the primacy of the first choosing
should not obscure the significance of the second. Because
Israel has entered into the covenant and its promises, she is
a coworker with Yahweh in bringing the promises to fulfillment: man is responsible for history. This sense of responsibility is pointed to at the end of the creation story in Genesis
1: "God said to them, 'Be fruitful and multiply, and fill the
earth and subdue it; and have dominion over the fish of
the sea and over the birds of the air and over every living
thing that moves upon the earth'" (Gen. 1:28). Although
man is a creature of Yahweh, nevertheless he is lord of the
earth. Moreover, when the story is read in context, it is also

being said that man is to bring all of creation to acknowl-
edge the sovereignty of Yahweh. The same position, in a
much more developed and explicitly historical form, is
stated again and again in the Deuteronomic interpretation
of history,[19] in the successive prophets, and later in the
various expectations as to the part man will play in help-
ing to usher in the messianic age. Although the position
is subject to idolatrous distortion, nevertheless it is man,
and specifically Israel, who is "to be the priestly mediator-
people of the age of salvation [Is. 61:6–9], the inheritrix
of the gracious promises to David [Is. 55:3f.], and the
guide of the nations to a right knowledge to God [Zech.
2:14f.; Is. 45:14]." [20] All of this takes place within the
grace of history, which is of God; nevertheless, man, as
the covenant partner of God, is responsible for history.
He is responsible both in the sense that history comes into
being as a consequence of God's action and man's response
to that action; and also because it is man who bears the
responsibility for the continuing vitality of the tradition
which remembers what took place between God and man,
and which thus enables the historical perception of reality
to continue.

Up to this point we have focused upon the exodus as
the event which brings the myth of history into being. In
our discussion of that event, what we have said about
promise and fulfillment, God and history, and the significance of events for the myth of history, holds in a very
similar way for the Christian and the Jew. In short, both Jew
and Christian accept the myth of history, and "the basic
language of Israel, given content by a certain group of
events . . . and derived from the political, legal, and
social spheres, is the basic language of the Church also." [21]

In regard to the responsibility of man for history, however, the Old and the New Israel take significantly diverging
paths. This divergence takes place because of the event of
the life, death, and resurrection of Jesus. Since it is an event

which brings about this divergence, and indeed an event
which would be incomprehensible apart from the exodus,
the change takes place as one which is already caught up
in the myth of history. However, the myth of history is
significantly changed, for now the controlling influence of
the exodus is replaced by the event of Jesus. In Karl Barth's
words, "since God Himself has become man, man is the
measure of all things." [22] Or, as Owen Barfield so beauti-
fully and provocatively expresses it: "[within Israel] a man
was born who simultaneously identified himself with, and
carefully distinguished himself from, the Creator of the world
—whom he called the Father. On the one hand: 'I am not
alone, but I and the Father that sent me,' etc. On the other:
'I and the Father are one,' etc. In one man the inwardness
of the Divine Name had been fully realized; the final participation, whereby man's Creator speaks from within man
himself, had been accomplished. The Word had been made
flesh." [23]

This event, then, speaks decisively not only about who
God is, but also as to who man is. Christians confess that
in this event perfect humanity is manifested for the first
time; that the manifestation of the whole nature of man
has taken place in history; and through our participation
in this event we come to know most fully the meaning of
human, historical existence. Man is not only lord of the
creation as in the old covenant, but is now seen in a
radically new way as the means whereby everything is led
into the New Creation. "For the creation waits with eager
longing for the revealing of the Sons of God . . . because
the creation itself will be set free from its bondage to decay
and obtain the glorious liberty of the children of God"
(Rom. 8:19, 21). Because man is "in Christ," he has been
empowered to play the decisive part in the divine plan for
the world. It is not too much to say that man, while remaining a creature, has been brought to share in divinity,
in creatorhood, and consequently in responsibility for the

history of the world. (In Eliade's terms, man has become a "Supernatural.") Man holds and exercises this responsibility in a manner analogous (no more, but no less) to the way the Christ possessed his own proper authority; namely, as claiming and "having nothing, and yet possessing everything" (II Cor. 6:10). This estimate of man certainly has its roots in Judaism. Yet, as a result of the event of Jesus, and of the reflection of the early Church upon that event, the high responsibility which came to be assigned to man was totally unacceptable to Judaism; and it remains unacceptable to the present day. That this was so during Jesus' own life is reflected in the controversy resulting from Jesus' placing not only the necessities, but also the passing needs, of man above the law; for example, the hunger of the disciples on the Sabbath, which they could have tolerated until sundown without heroic sacrifice (Mark 2:23ff.).

The event of Jesus, moreover, did not only result in making man the measure of all things. If man is lifted by the Christ to so high a position of responsibility, then the consequences of any fall from this height become correspondingly more severe. Seeing himself as the beneficiary of such an act of grace, man's sense of what he loses by any rebellious abdication of this responsibility becomes correspondingly radical. Neither existentially nor logically can the radical awareness of the irresponsibility of sin be understood apart from the understanding of the radical responsibility conferred by grace. Thus, if the Jew does not know the exalted responsibility conferred upon man by the Incarnation, neither does he know of the radical sense of alienation from God which ensues when man sinfully renounces that responsibility. In this matter the language of the Old and the New Testaments is related, but it is not the same.

The Christian awareness of his own sin, therefore, is the negative testimony to his responsibility for history and for the creation: the creation, which is now seen as being within the historical order, and which, together with man, "waits" for its redemption within that order. In Friedrich Gogarten's exposition of the nature of historical existence and its relation to the Christian faith, it is above all else in the Christian's understanding of himself as sinner that he acknowledges himself as responsible for history; and hence it is this self-understanding which is so essential for history.[24]

Thus, when reality is understood as historical, man is aware of his responsibility for history: positively in his role as the recipient of the gift of grace and lordship, and negatively in his role as the guilty rebel who wants to understand his own responsibility only as responsibility to himself alone. Positively and negatively, however, the understanding of reality as historical includes the self-understanding that one is responsible for history. This self-understanding is not a moral addendum, but an integral part of living within the myth of history.

THE ORIGINAL RELATIONAL EVENT

In our discussion of the origin of the myth of history we have placed the event of the exodus and the event of Jesus at the center of the myth of history, according the latter event the primacy and hence the control of the myth of history. Since we have placed this emphasis upon these events, it is appropriate that we elaborate our understanding of their character.

In *I and Thou,* Martin Buber states how this matter stands in terms which are perfectly applicable to Christianity, and ideally suited to our purposes here. In a characteristically concise way he declares: "Every great culture that comprehends nations rests on an original relational incident, on a response to the *Thou* made at its source, on an act of the being made by the spirit." [25]

Here Buber has in mind as his model the exodus, the "journey in the course of which the [Hebrew] Nation came into being." [26] This is also of the greatest significance to us

as Christians, although now in a new way due to the event
of Jesus, as a result of which the New Israel has come into
being. In both cases, however, it is a meeting in which a
new relationship is initiated. This relationship becomes the
source of the being and the determinant of the activity of
all those who are in this relationship. In Buber's terms,
this is the I-Thou relationship upon which all other relationships and activities depend. Jews know this encounter,
this personal relationship, to be with Yahweh; for Christians he is the Father of Our Lord Jesus Christ. In either
case, and here the distinctive character of the biblical myth
emerges, it is in a concrete and particular incident that God
manifests his Spirit, and to which the spirit of man responds.
(Parenthetically, it is this incident-centered aspect of
Buber's formulation which would call for modification before it would be applicable to other religions and the cultures to which they have given rise.)

Among the various reasons why Buber's way of expressing this commends itself to us is the fact that it calls our
attention to the essential role which language plays in the
whole process. It is language, the saying of "Thou," which
brings relationship into being; and the continuation of this
relationship is dependent upon the creative phenomenon
of language. Buber writes: "I become through my relation
to the *Thou;* as I become *I,* I say *Thou.*" [27] Here, of course,
language is not conceived of rationalistically as a process
in which events and things are "tagged" with arbitrarily
chosen syllables. Rather, the word of God's promise and the
word of man's response bring the event or relationship into
being, and this relationship cannot be conceived of apart
from this speaking. The word comes into being with the
event, and the event comes into being with the word. In
Vico's terms, the nature of the word is nothing but its coming into being at certain times and in certain fashions:
it is word event (see Chapter 2). "When [*Thou*] is spoken,"
says Buber, "the speaker enters the word and takes his
stand in it." [28] This original creative encounter and con-

versation, "strengthened by the similarly directed power of succeeding generations, creates in the spirit a special conception of the cosmos." [29] Out of the continually renewed relationship to this original relational event, man finds the power and courage to "build again and again, in a special conception of space, dwellings for God and dwellings for men, and fill swaying time with new hymns and new songs, and shape the very community of men." [30]

Very briefly, this is Buber's understanding of the relationship between God and man, and between revelation and culture. This relationship will be the underlying concern of this entire book, for we take this to be the fundamental issue being discussed not only in terms of the relationship between history and theology, but also in terms of such related theological controversies as demythologization, the "secularization of the gospel," the "new hermeneutic," and so on.

There are, admittedly, certain inconsistencies in the central argument found in *I and Thou*. The mystery of human experience and sin enables us to be consistently certain that all arguments are inconsistent to some degree.[31] Buber's inconsistencies do not, however, affect the essential validity of his understanding of the origin of culture. His position in this matter, like all "positions," is not unique with him. It does, however, possess several very attractive aspects. Important among these is the fact that it is the work of an author who is widely known and respected beyond strictly theological circles; that it is expressed concisely, yet richly, in language which transcends any one confessional or school position; and, above all, it is set forth in language which particularly lends itself to comprehending and, hopefully, advancing what we take to be the central issues in the recent discussion of the relationship between theology and history.

For these reasons, Buber's analysis is accepted here at the beginning of this book as being congruent with our own, and frequent reference will be made to it during the development of our discussion. We understand Buber to be saying that it is the original relational event which gives us our fundamental view or picture of the world and of our own personal and social being within that world. Further, we understand this to mean that the special problems of theoretical and practical life all take their particular forms by segregation out of the total picture given to us in the original relational event, and that these various forms retain their vitality only insofar as they preserve their connection with the event, and with each other within the event.[32] Moreover, we understand this analysis to apply to historical consciousness and inquiry in even its most "secular" forms. More specifically, the concept of "history" as it is commonly understood today is founded upon the original relational event of the exodus, and subsequently of Jesus; and "history" retains the vitality which it possesses because of the power of the original relational event which is carried within that concept.

AN END TO HISTORY VERSUS MYTH

We have argued that the myth of history is equally integral both to biblical religion and to our contemporary historical consciousness; and that this is so in spite of the fact that in the latter there is not characteristically any recognition that history is of God. The reformulation of the understanding of history which we are suggesting, asks, of course, that both historians and theologians take the category of myth into their thinking in a positive way. This suggestion will initially win, in all probability, only the enmity of the many historians and theologians who see the issues simply in terms of history versus myth. Nevertheless, we have indicated, and this will be developed in detail in the following chapters, why we believe that our reformulation of this matter is superior to that which is demonstrated in the familiar history-versus-myth polarity and polemics.

Attempting to speak only from the point of view of the Church, we would say that the first step in the reformulation which is being suggested is the acceptance by Christianity of the category of myth. This acceptance should not be made grudgingly, but humbly, wholeheartedly, and joyously. Formally described, myth is for Christianity what it is for other religions: "the account of what has befallen." [33] "Let all the house of Israel therefore know assuredly that God has made him both Lord and Christ, this Jesus whom you crucified" (Acts 2:36). The myth of Christianity tells of what befell at the point in history at which it came into being, and it receives its classical formulation in the New Testament kerygma.

This admission of the mythic character of Christianity is not one which attempts to make a virtue out of a necessity, nor is it a retreat in any sense. Moreover, it is not really a novelty in Christian thought; rather, it arises out of a renewed appreciation of mythic thought. As a result of a century of accumulated scholarship in a variety of fields, we know that myth does not refer essentially to "fables," imaginary stories about the gods, ostensibly historical stories purporting to explain natural phenomena, and so on. When the members of a society accepted a myth they did not understand that myth in any such way but, rather, as a true story of what had befallen them; a story growing out of the encounter with the holy; a story which manifests the true nature of the world, and which is therefore the basis for relating oneself and one's society to the world. Myth gives to its adherent his first principles; or, in contemporary terminology, his "ultimate concern."

This formal definition of myth fits the Christian kerygma perfectly. For Christians, the story about Jesus the Christ is the true story arising out of our encounter with Jesus the Christ, a story which tells us who we are and which gives us our first principles and our view of the world. The Christian has no reason to be embarrassed that the kerygma

is, when *formally* described, indistinguishable from a large
body of other myths. The Christian is indeed different from
the rest of mankind, but this distinctiveness does not lie in
his possessing some unique capacity for apprehending God's
disclosure of himself. (The operation of the Holy Spirit is
not confined to the Old and the New Israel.) The Christian
confesses what has befallen him, bets his life upon that
confession and, insofar as his sinful nature permits, is will-
ing to see through a glass darkly until the consummation.
Nothing has happened to the Christian which takes him out
of the situation in which the Creator has placed the creature. Not the least of the benefits of the admission of this
situation would be our deliverance from the tenuous, tedious polemics which seek to make a radical separation between "historical" Christianity and "mythological" religions.

If the Christian faith cannot be distinguished from all
other religions upon the basis of its being nonmythic in
character, how shall we account for its distinctiveness?
The answer, of course, is that Christianity receives its distinctive character from the peculiar characteristics of the
myth out of which it arises and lives. There is no one
correct way to describe the rich and complex myth or
picture of the world which informs Christianity. The description which we will make, however, can be pointed to
concisely with the phrase: "Reality is conceived of historically." This is perhaps *the* characterization of the mythic
picture of Christianity for our time.

Having laid these foundations, we would wish to turn
to the early Councils of the Church in order to show how
the myth of history was worked out in terms of the discussions of the person of Jesus the Christ. The limited scope
of this book precludes that, however, and the next focus
for our attention must be the first *self-conscious* and *systematic* attempts to understand experience in historical
terms. This means, inevitably, that we must turn to the work
of Giambattista Vico.

2

Giambattista Vico and the Modern Historical Consciousness

The attempt to date the beginning of something so elusive as a new set of ideas, or a new attitude toward experience, is always arbitrary to some extent. Where shall we locate the emergence of our modern historical consciousness, with its self-conscious awareness of man as a peculiarly historical being who is continually creating himself in the historical process? One might make a case of the time of the Reformation, with its frequent rejection of tradition and authority, and its turning in a critical spirit to original documents in order to see what man had created in history. We believe, however, that it is more helpful to place the emergence of the modern historical consciousness at a later period: at the end of the seventeenth and the beginning of the eighteenth centuries. It is most misleading to locate in this period the origin of the historical understanding of reality, for that understanding arose out of the biblical experience which we have described in the preceding chapter.[1] However, during this period there does arise for the first time a *self-conscious, systematic,* and *critical* approach to historical reality. History now becomes, partly in reaction to the profound impact of the ahistorical philosophy of René Descartes (1596–1650), self-consciously aware of itself as a distinctive and appropriately systematic mode of knowl-

33

edge, with its own peculiar capacity for the critical handling
of evidence. Admittedly, this new orientation to history par-
took to some extent of the Cartesianism against which it
was a reaction. Nevertheless, it was a revolt by a perceptive
few who supported Western man's historical sense against
the abstract, ahistorical Cartesian rationalism that had
swept Europe.[2] The profound effect of this revolt upon the
study of history, the Church and its theology, and the whole
modern spirit is our legacy today.

Certainly the outstanding characteristic of this new approach to history is the *self-conscious* awareness that man
is responsible for the world, and that he is actively engaged
in creating and testing meaning for his personal and social
life. Man stands in the center of the world; he is in a very
real sense a creator; he creates for himself, and he should
attend to that which he has created. In Eliade's terms, man
becomes a "Supernatural"; or, at least, takes on many of
the characteristics associated with the "Supernaturals."

This orientation to experience carries with it a fundamental methodological principle: authority and tradition
are not self-validating. Man has created authorities, traditions, and systems of all kinds; but, since they are human
creations, they are always open to critical evaluation, and
possible reconstruction or rejection, as history proceeds into
the future. If man's creations were to be removed from the
judgment of future history, this would be to break the
promise-fulfillment tension and, with it, the myth of history.
Or, traditionally: man is not to be permitted to idolize his
own creations. Man, as a true creator, may make new creations in order to arrive at new ends of his own choosing. In
all of this we see an obvious, although not complete, parallel
with the developing interest in natural science during the
same period. In both areas, as we would expect, this new
orientation to experience is developed gropingly, tenta-
tively, and often with (to us) bizarre mistakes. Once the
process started, however, there was no turning back. One
"inviolable" area after another gave way under the impact

of history and science. This was the inexorable result of the
basic insight that man has created his world, and has created
it for himself.

This development contained within it a fundamental and
seemingly unavoidable ambiguity. One aspect of the development is that it "already contained the outlines of
secularism: the world resting on itself, containing within
itself its own law and bearing within itself its own truth
and justification. . . . [here] 'Man encounters only himself.' " [3] The concept of the "secular" is, notoriously, a difficult one in contemporary discussion.[4] This difficulty in
language reflects the more general difficulty which we are
having in coming to a new understanding of ourselves and
our world. If "secular" means a radical concern for and
attentiveness toward the "this-worldly," then it follows from
what we have said earlier that both history and the Christian
faith are profoundly and properly secular. Indeed, secularism understood in this sense derives in very large part from
the biblical myth of history. It is not this sense of the secular which we wish to discuss here, however.

Secularism may also mean something quite distinct from
"this-worldliness"; namely, the affirmation of a *reality* in
which we find our existence, and which is self-sufficient,
self-explanatory, and all-encompassing.[5] Since this reality is
self-sufficient, such categories as "relationship," "speaking,"
and the "future" (the "new") are foreign to it. Since this
reality is self-explanatory, the encounter with it is characteristically marked by the perception of the "clear and distinct
idea." Hence the precision of "seeing" is appropriate to this
reality, and not the ambiguity, the surprise, and the unknown future opened up through the act of "speaking." Further, since this reality is self-sufficient and self-explanatory,
the attitude of thankfulness for this reality is unnecessary, if
not inappropriate. Finally, since this reality is all-encompassing, any other interpretation of experience must be
overtly or covertly opposed.

Our discussion of the myth of history in Chapter 1 makes

it clear that the concept of the secular in this second sense is completely foreign to biblical and historical experience. The victory of secularism in this second sense would only mean the end of the myth of history and the historical perception of experience.[6] Nevertheless, the influence of this form of secularism was to be found in the development of our modern historical consciousness. The preoccupation of many modern historians with the objective (clear and distinct) fact, with all of its overtones of self-sufficiency and staticness, is one significant indication that this is so. Moreover, this situation was recognized from the beginning of the modern period, as we shall see in our discussion of Giambattista Vico.

This is one aspect of the development of our modern historical consciousness. The other aspect, and hence the ambiguity of the development, is that this secularization of history has been consistently opposed or undercut by historians themselves. In part this took place through the articulate and self-conscious opposition of such men as Vico. (This does not mean that Vico was *completely* free of the secularism which we have discussed, but that he saw and attempted to counter the secular, or antihistorical, aspect of modern historical consciousness.) In greater part, however, the undercutting of the secularization of history is to be found in the thought of those very persons who were seemingly caught up in an unreflective secularization of history. This is true, in spite of the fact that they did not themselves recognize their opposition. This unrecognized opposition resides in the continuing adherence to the myth of history by all historians. A sincere lip service may be paid to the "objective facts" and the "clear and distinct ideas" of history, but this normally has not seriously compromised a basic adherence to the myth of history. Thus, historians may declare that no area is exempt from man's critical evaluation; but this does not hold for the dominant affirmation of the historian: History is the true story of human experience. This affirmation has been, and largely continues to be, exempt from the principle that everything is open to the judgment and control of critical thought. Indeed, the unreflective and pragmatic character of the modern spirit has prevented a widespread self-consciousness about the myth of history and the special status which it enjoys. *Within* the context of the myth of history, it is both possible and legitimate (as we shall discuss more fully in our examination of the theology of Rudolf Bultmann in Chapter 3) to abstract and isolate "objective facts" for purposes of intensive examination and control. The thisworldly character of the myth of history encourages this very process of abstraction. However, such abstraction depends upon the myth of history, and not vice versa. (The correctness of this assertion is supported by the observation that only those civilizations which participate in the myth of history become preoccupied with "objective facts.") It is the reality of the myth of history, for all its lack of self-sufficiency, clarity, objectivity, etc., that has captured the minds and imaginations of historians. Consequently, as we discussed before, such historians as Barbara Tuchman may declare that objective historical facts exist independently of the historian; but, fortunately, they do not write history as if this were so! One of the purposes of this whole inquiry is to work toward the resolution of these ambiguities and confusions in the modern historical consciousness.

GIAMBATTISTA VICO

It will be helpful to illustrate and develop this brief general analysis of the character of the modern historical consciousness through an examination of the work of a specific representative of this tradition during the period of its inception. Among the earliest group of men who gave systematic expression to this new self-consciousness about history, and certainly the most impressive of these, was the Neapolitan,

Giambattista Vico (1668–1744). In Vico "we reach for the first time," in R. G. Collingwood's judgment, "a completely modern idea of what the subject-matter of history is. . . . like God Himself, [man] is a real creator, bringing into existence both form and matter . . . in the corporate work of his own historical development." [7] Not only did Vico reach this understanding, but, as we shall see, he developed it in such a way as to provide the ground-plan for a whole mode of thinking.[8] For these reasons, we wish to examine Vico's major work, *The New Science*.[9] This examination will reveal two organically related aspects of his work. First, against the background of Cartesian rationalism against which Vico was in revolt, we will examine Vico's theory as to how historical knowledge is possible, and how language and myth play a critical role in the process of arriving at historical knowledge. This aspect of Vico's thought has an interesting and significant relation both to what we have said earlier concerning myth and the original relational event, and to what we want to say about the contemporary discussion of the relationship between myth, language, history, and theology. Second, having set forth Vico's theory of historical knowledge, we will then examine in greater detail what he has to say concerning language. In this examination we will look most specifically at his concept of poetry and symbol, their truthful character, and the methodological implications of all of this for the study of history. Concerning the methodological aspects of Vico's theory, we would like to stress their organic relationship with the more strictly theoretical considerations in *The New Science*. This close relationship is a result of the fact that the capacity for historical inquiry is not primarily a matter of possessing an appropriate technique. What is primary, rather, is the appropriate attitude toward what we now call history, namely, being inwardly convinced that history is a source of meaning; and, in consequence, being able to be attentive to what takes place in history.[10] In our own terminology, this attitude toward history is an expression of one's participation in the myth of history. Once this attitude has been reached, it is then implemented by means of an appropriate technique arising out of it. The subsequent successful application of the technique to specific problems in turn reinforces the historical understanding of reality upon which the technique is based. Thus, as we shall see, Vico arrives at the conclusion that our chief source of knowledge is the study of what man has made (that is, history), that the primary thing which man has made is language, and that therefore if one is to be a historian one must develop a technique of "etymological analysis" which will permit him to be attentive to the history of language. In this way, historical understanding and historical technique always remain in the closest relationship. A consequence of this has been that, in the field of history, there has been no development paralleling the development in the natural sciences whereby technology and technicians have an important and semiautonomous position.

With these preliminary remarks in mind, let us now turn to Vico's *New Science*. The development of Vico's thought in *The New Science* can best be understood against the background of the thinker with whom he saw himself in conflict. For Vico the opponent was René Descartes (1596–1650), whose thought had been so successful in captivating Vico's contemporaries. Descartes brought to a focus, and thereby advanced, the ahistorical thinking which had never been absent from European thought. Although the explicit subject-object formulation of the problem of knowledge was to come only later with Kant and Coleridge, this problem was the substance of Descartes's concern; a concern which was primarily epistemological, and only secondarily ontological or metaphysical.[11] Descartes's chief criterion of truth is that judgments claiming it must consist of clear and distinct ideas. "I call that clear," says Descartes in *Principles of Philosophy*, "which is present and

apparent to an attentive mind, in the same way as we
assert that we see objects clearly when, being present to the
beholding eye, they operate upon it with sufficient strength.
But the distinct is that which is so precise and different from
all other objects that it contains within itself nothing but
what is clear." [12] In this understanding of the characteristics
of genuine knowledge we note the emphasis upon seeing
(rather than hearing), clarity, precision, simplicity, operation, and (by implication) control. Mathematical knowledge immediately suggests itself as the clearest example of
this understanding of knowledge. It is especially significant
for our purposes that Descartes goes on to maintain that his
theory of knowledge necessitates proving the existence of a
God, but a God who has a very limited relation to that
addressing, revealing, and yet hidden God who reigns in the
history recorded in the Old and New Testaments. "By the
name God," says Descartes in his third "Meditation," "I
understand a substance which is infinite, independent, all-
knowing, all-powerful and by which I myself and everything else . . . have been created." [13]

In developing his thought along these lines, Descartes
consistently, explicitly, and contemptuously ruled out precisely those unclear and indistinct ideas (by Descartes's
standards) upon which history depends: memories, motives,
inner psychic states, images and symbols, works of art with
their kaleidoscopic possibilities of meaning, and so on. In
contemporary terms, Descartes rejected the whole realm of
personal knowledge, the world of I-Thou; and he supported
this rejection with "the unparalleled successes of the new
physico-mathematical sciences, the nearest approximation
to infallible knowledge of natural facts to which man had
yet attained." [14]

Vico perceived that Descartes left no room for history.
Vico, however, since he was convinced that history was a
necessary and possible form of knowledge, began to work
toward a new theory of knowledge which would show the

validity of historical knowledge. His first step in this program was his Inaugural Lecture of 1710, delivered to the University of Naples. This lecture, entitled *De antiquissima Italorum sapienta* ("Ancient Wisdom of the Italians"), was an audacious, thoroughgoing attack upon the Cartesian position. Vico began his attack by asking what it is that makes mathematical ideas, the prime example of Descartes's clear and distinct ideas, so irrefutable. Vico's answer, first fully stated in his "Ancient Wisdom of the Italians," is that the clarity and irrefutable character of mathematical propositions derives from the fact that we ourselves have made them. In geometry we are able to demonstrate truth because we have created it.[15] This is the meaning of Vico's famous formula, the central principle of the "Ancient Wisdom of the Italians": *Verum et factum convertuntur* ("The true [*verum*] and the made [*factum*] are convertible").[16] This situation, of course, is to some extent the case in respect to any human creation. We can, however, only *fully* create, and hence *fully* know, when we make or design something literally out of nothing. And, says Isaiah Berlin in a nice summary of Vico on this matter, "This is virtually the case with algebra and arithmetic. The shapes of the symbols, auditory or visual, that we employ, are made of sense-given material. But they are arbitrarily chosen, and are used as counters in a game that we ourselves have freely invented." [17] Consequently, Vico concedes to Descartes the truth and the especial clarity and convincing power of mathematical propositions, but points out that this privileged position rests upon their being arbitrary human creations.

Having granted Descartes's position, but at the same time appropriately qualifying and limiting it, Vico's next step was to set out the theoretical basis for historical knowledge. As Berlin points out in his incisive description of Vico's intellectual development, Vico did this by denying that knowledge could be exhaustively divided into three kinds:

rational intuition, as in metaphysics; deductive knowledge,
as in mathematics; and empirical knowledge, as in the
natural sciences. There is, in addition, a fourth kind of
knowledge. This is self-knowledge:

. . . knowledge of situations in which we, the knowing sub-
jects, are ourselves the actors, endowed with motives, purposes
and a continuous life, which we understand, as it were, from
inside; here and only here, we are not passive observers looking
on from the outside, as when we contemplate the external
world, where all that we can see are events, or the surfaces of
things, about the inner lives or goals of which—or whether, indeed, they have, or in principle could be said to have, goals, or
inner lives—we can only darkly speculate.[18]

This self-knowledge, which Vico equates with historical
knowledge in its broadest sense, is a distinct and necessary
form of knowledge. Since I have not made myself, self-
knowledge does not have the clear and distinct quality of
mathematics; but neither does it have mathematics' "game"
quality of "fictitiousness" and arbitrariness. Even more significantly, this self-knowledge is "superior" to the empirical
knowledge of the natural sciences because it is not an observing and organizing of phenomena which are exterior
to, and finally unknowable by, ourselves.[19] In self-knowledge we can know ourselves, and others by analogy with
ourselves, through the examination of ourselves. This examination takes place primarily through the examination
of what has been produced in history, that is, the customs,
the deeds and, above all, the language of men. All of this
Vico refers to as the *certum,* that is, the "cultural residue,"
which is the subject matter of the historian.[20] But, Vico goes
on, we must not stop here. It is crucial that the records of
history (the *certum*) be understood as that which man has
made (the *factum*). The *certum* and the *factum* are convertible; or, less technically, history leads to knowledge,
and specifically self-knowledge, when it approaches its

documents (the *certum*) with the understanding that these are what other selves have created in history (the *factum*).[21]

When man creates in history, then, and above all when he creates language, he creates a structure that constitutes an interpretation of his experience which organizes the world around him. The study of history is the ongoing understanding and evaluation (in effect, a reinterpretation) of these interpretive structures which men have created.

In Berlin's judgment, "History for him [Vico] is the orderly procession of ever deepening types of apprehension of the world, of ways of feeling, acting, expressing, each of which grows out of, and supersedes, its predecessor." [22] Vico's stress upon the ongoing development of history is one in which the legacy of the past is taken with complete seriousness, but without obscuring either the necessity of reapprehending the past in ways appropriate to the present, or the necessity of leaving the future free to apprehend the past in ways which are perhaps as yet unthinkable.

With this understanding of history, Vico attempted in his day to oppose the claim that the "clear and distinct idea" constitutes the highest form of knowledge, and that therefore history must be approached in terms of a clearly and distinctly apprehended "hard core of historical fact." However, in Vico's day as in our own, the "hard core of historical fact," the "brute facts," and all that such expressions imply, are difficult to eradicate because they carry some of the authority of Descartes's clear and distinct ideas. Although the "hard core of historical fact" has neither the beautiful simplicity and clarity, nor the total abstractness, nor the usefulness of the mathematical idea, it is, nevertheless, similar to the mathematical idea in that it is an abstraction which we have arbitrarily created (in this case, out of the complex flow of history), and which we can use as a counter "in a game that we ourselves have freely invented." The moving of abstract counters in freely invented games gives a sense of control and calls for a very limited commitment on the part of the player. Consequently, attempts to think in terms of "hard-core facts" have a very wide appeal. This appeal constitutes part of the limited usefulness of the concept of hard-core facts. However, a difficulty, which does not have a real parallel in mathematics, arises when the fallacious assumption is made that the hard-core facts exist objectively "out there," and constitute the substance of history. Vico, in his day, was trying to eradicate this fallacy by insisting upon the conversion of the *certum* with the *factum,* i.e., the study of history (the *certum*) is a reinterpretation of those interpretative structures (the *factum*) which man has created. Or, more elegantly, Vico was affirming: "The spirit is never alien to the forms of its own creativity and the products which this creativity has brought forth. Thus is established the . . . conversion . . . of the 'certum' with the 'factum,' and by this conversion, the reunion of the spirit with itself in its documents." [23]

Thus the formula which Vico applied to mathematics, "the true and the made are convertible," he finds may also apply to history. When it is applied to history, however, a different kind of knowledge arises from that when it is applied to mathematics. In the case of mathematics, as we have seen, the resulting knowledge is clear and distinct; but it is also "fictitious" and "arbitrary." In history it must be otherwise, however, for unlike mathematics we have not created ourselves and our world out of nothing. Consequently, history does not yield clear and distinct ideas. Rather, history deals with the heritage of the past, understanding for the present, and hope for the future; which is to say, history deals with the tangled but nonfictitious ("true") matters of purpose, goal, motive, acts of will, fear, hope and so on, in its effort to arrive at self-knowledge. "Self-knowledge thus stands halfway between deductive or formal knowledge of pure artifacts [for example, mathematics], and inductive or perceptual knowledge of given, irremovable, opaque 'brute' Nature." [24]

What, then, is the relationship between what man makes

in history, and the truth of self-knowledge which comes about through the study of what he has made? Vico answers this concisely in his statement: "The nature of institutions [*verum*] is nothing but their coming into being (*nascimento*) at certain times and in certain guises [*factum*]." [25] Less concisely, the nature or truth about "institutions" (e.g., language, myth, religion, the state, the family, the arts, etc.) is to be discovered through the analysis of how, respectively, they came into being—and including an analysis of how the various transformations of these institutions came into being. This knowledge is knowledge of history, that is, knowledge of the *factum* which man has created; and, as such, this is self-knowledge. Or, the truth of self-knowledge is convertible with what man has made in history.

We are not accustomed to speaking of this matter in terms of *verum* and *factum,* but in terms of *content* and *form*. Using the latter set of terms, Vico is saying that the content of anything is "nothing but" the form which it assumed at the point in history at which it came into being. (This is an early version of "the medium is the message"!) Content comes into existence with, or within, form. Consequently, content and form (*verum* and *factum*) may be distinguished, but they cannot be discussed adequately in isolation from one another. To know one is to know the other; the two are convertible: *Verum et factum convertuntur*. Negatively, content and form arise together, and will not yield to the separation attempted when one speaks, for example, of the inner meaning of myths; or of fact *and* interpretation in the study of history. Thinking in terms of that most fundamental creation of man—myth—we would say with Caponigri: "Myth and idea [*factum* and *verum*] stand in a relationship of tension and dialectic, which is the most intimate and self-generative process of the human subject." [26] Myth, as Vico clearly understood, is a story in which is expressed the way in which man encounters, understands, and interacts with his world.

That these original, mythically expressed encounters are

largely personal in nature is reflected in Vico's repeated
statements that the poetic images found in the myths are
"for the most part of animated beings, of gods or heroes."
Since language and myth arise in the process of articulating
and hence interpreting these encounters, the later analysis
of language and myth (the *factum*) is the primary instrument which enables us to reapprehend the reality of the
original relational event, and to come to know the nature
of that which came into being *with* the poetic images. Here
the word "with" is emphasized, for prior to the creation or
coming into being of the image (word), man does not know
the reality which confronts him; nor does he know his own
reality in regard to this confrontation. Prior to the word,
nothing is made and nothing is known. As Caponigri points
out, the poetic word or myth is an ontological structure
because its creation is "an act by which the human spirit
generates or creates its own being . . . [and] the act by
which it generates its own presence to itself, and in that
presence, its whole being as spirit." [27] Thus the poetic creation is the "constitutive act of human consciousness and of
the world which it invokes and in which it dwells; it establishes, as it were, the ontology of that world." [28]

The search for self-knowledge through the study of what
man has made is, Vico recognizes, a "Godlike" activity. In
this activity man perceives what he has created as well as
who he is as the creator of history and, in a very real sense,
of his world. Moreover, man also perceives himself to be the
sustainer of history, for it continues only because man is
attentive to history. In Buber's words, it is only "through the
similarly directed power of succeeding generations" that
historical attentiveness, understanding, and traditions are
sustained, recreated, and developed.

These are the main outlines of Vico's theory of historical
knowledge, including some indication of the role of myth
and language; a theory which was both prompted by Vico's
historical studies and suited to their further advance. Ac-

cording to this theory, man's social beginnings are associated with encounters with his environment, out of which there arose by necessity primitive poetic images, images which were an integral part of that encounter. Thus Vico understands man in terms of history; man cannot be comprehended apart from the self-knowledge which comes to expression in the creations (the *factum*) of history. If we are to know ourselves, then we must be attentive to history. Indeed, in a diffuse way, Vico is saying repeatedly that while mathematics describes a fictitious world, and natural science an opaque one, history presents us with the true story of the real world.[29] Vico, who was among the first to "break" myths while *at the same time* taking what they are saying with complete seriousness, had his own myth: History presents us with the true story of reality.[30] In other words, Vico used the myth of history to reinterpret the other myths or interpretive schemes (e.g., that of Descartes) which he encountered. In doing this, Vico was continuing, in a new form, a process which has usually characterized the evangelical efforts of both the Old and the New Israel, as, for example, in the attacks of Israel upon the baalim of the Canaanites and the attacks of the Church upon the mystery religions of the Hellenistic world. The same process continues to take place in our own day, with whatever imperfections, in terms of the demythologization controversy and its sequels (see Chapter 3).

LANGUAGE AND HISTORY

We have seen the importance of what man has made (the *factum*) for Vico's theory of historical knowledge, and how the primary thing which man has made is language. Language is the medium in which thought generally, and man's image of himself and his world in particular, are formed and recorded. History, the study of what man has made, is therefore, first of all, the study of language. Vico

develops his whole theory and methodology of historical
knowledge in terms of language; it is the study of language
which enables him to be attentive to history. Because of
this centrality of language and history for Vico, and because
his discussion of language and history has remarkable and
illuminating parallels with much contemporary theological
discussion of language, myth, and hermeneutic, it will be
worthwhile to set forth in greater detail Vico's ideas about
language.

Vico's concern for language manifests itself at the very
beginning of *The New Science*. In his introduction to *The
New Science*, entitled "The Idea of the Work," we find an
extended explanation of the strange and complex allegorical
picture which appears as the frontispiece to the work. In
this explanation, Vico announces his discovery that the
early peoples "were poets who spoke in poetic characters,"
and that this discovery of the "primary operation of the
human mind" is "the master key of this Science." [31] With the
aid of this key Vico plans to show us "the beginnings of
the humanity of the nations." [32]

When Vico says that early peoples were poets, he means
that they were creators (ποειν, to create); and above all
else, they were the creators of language. Vico speaks of this
creation of language in terms of the creation of "sublime
fables," "wholly corporeal" (or concrete and nondiscursive)
in character. The "poetic characters" constitute the essence
of these fables created by the "spontaneous consciousness"
of man.[33] These poetic characters, frequently characterized
as "true narration" (*vera narratio*), are inherently necessary productions of human nature, and consist of "certain
imaginative genera (images for the most part of animated
substances, of gods or heroes, formed by their imagination). . . ." [34]

Out of this basic human phenomenon of language expressed in the fables, Vico maintains somewhat obscurely,
there developed allegory, mythology and, finally, ety-

mology. Allegories took the "imaginative class concepts" found in the fables, and gave them a "univocal significa- tion connoting a quality common to all their species and individuals (as Achilles connotes an idea of valour com- mon to all strong men . . .)." [35] Allegory is defined by Vico as *diversiloquium* because allegories signify and ex- plicate in one general concept the diverse species of men, deeds, or things found within the fables.[36] Vico makes no clear distinction between allegory and mythology. Myth, like fable, is defined as *vera narratio,* or true narration, "the natural speech which . . . had been spoken in the world at one time"; [37] and mythologies are a form of allegory which are the "proper language" of the fables.[38]

If the differences between allegory and mythology are vague, when Vico comes to etymology he makes a relatively clear distinction. Etymology, the chief critical instrument of *The New Science,* is a later, self-conscious, and more sys- tematic development than allegory and mythology. More important, however, is the fact that etymology, as Vico con- ceives of it, is essentially like allegory and mythology be- cause it takes the poetically produced word or image or fable as a "given," and then proceeds by analysis and reflec- tion to make explicit the various subtleties of meaning im- plicit within it. Vico was convinced that the poetic images could be treated in this way with fruitful results because he understood that the images, as part of the *factum* of his- tory, had not been created arbitrarily, but "had natural relations to the ideas they were meant to signify . . ."; [39] "they carried their meaning in themselves." [40] Thus Vico had the insight, rare in the eighteenth century, that names were not originally attached to persons or objects or events as a convenient and conventional tag, but that in the course of concrete historical development a name or image or symbol is created by, and stands for, a historically experi- enced reality. The name or symbol does not stand apart from the nature or reality which it signifies, as witness is

borne by the universal conservatism which people exhibit in
regard to changing their names.[41] Form and content are not
to be separated. Thus, the image of "sun" or "moon" is not
separate from the complex human experience of regularly
passing time, with its element of "growth," "life," "death,"
and so on, but, rather, participates in it as an integral part
of it. In contemporary terms, "sun" is a performatory word.
In this way we see, to draw upon a contemporary expression
of this point of view, that symbols are a necessary means not
only of opening up and dealing with "dimensions and elements of reality which otherwise would remain unapproach-
able," but also of unlocking "dimensions and elements of
our soul which correspond to the dimensions and elements
of reality." [42] It is because the "poetic images" have this
quality that allegory, mythology, and etymology may all
be understood as being forms of reflection upon the primary
words or images in order to arrive at the essential content
or meaning which they held for those who created them,
and which still inheres in them. Moreover, it is only when
these reflective processes of allegory, mythology, and etymology remain true to the primary poetic material upon
which they are based that they retain their character of
"true narration."

The way in which Vico attempts to argue for the "true"
character of the original poetic material ("myth" in our
own usage) seems naïve, at least at first sight.

Here emerges a great principle of human institutions, confirm-
ing the origin of poetry disclosed in this work: that since the
first men of the gentile world had the simplicity of children, who
are truthful by nature, the first fables could not feign anything
false; they must therefore have been, as they have been defined
above, true narrations.[43]

Vico's language is quaint, but the effect of his taking this
position is profound and far-reaching. In the judgment of

A. R. Caponigri, "poetic becomes the adjective by which he [Vico] designates and describes the whole pre-reflective life of man. . . . The forms of poetry are not the external encasement of the movements of unreflective life; they are its genuine incorporation and articulation and spring with complete necessity from the internal character of the movement of spontaneous consciousness." [44]

Three characteristics of Vico's position here call for particular attention. First, Vico establishes as fundamentally important the poetic production which came into being during the period of origin of a society or nation. Such productions are developed and refined in subsequent generations, but these developments are determined by, and must remain true to, the original poetic material. The close parallel here with Buber's idea of the "original relational incident" is evident. Second, this earliest, constitutive material is—in our contemporary terminology—a "language phenomenon." The imagination of these "first men" responded to their environment, and out of this interaction language arose, bringing to expression the reality they encountered in their environment. All that we can know of these men, their imagination and environment, we know only through the analysis of this language, and the language which developed out of it. Man's attentiveness to history is possible (in an instrumental sense) and productive primarily because of language. Vico expressed this as early as 1710, in his "Ancient Wisdom of the Italians," in words which sound remarkably contemporary: "Minds are formed by the character of language, not language by the minds of those who speak it." [45] Third, although we would not want to say that the "first men" were "truthful by nature," we do consistently say something which is basically very similar. Concerning the exodus, for example, we say that the various motifs ("escape," "covenant," "promise," and so on) which go to form the exodus narrative, were "true" for the community of Hebrews. While in some situations the

Hebrews were very adept at lying, the exodus was no lie.
It was the true story of the world as they encountered it, a
story arising out of the interaction between their imagination and their environment (the dominant feature of
which was Yahweh), and all coming to expression in the
language of escape and covenant and promised land.

Vico is the father of modern historiography, then, not
primarily because he developed a critical technique for
"doing" history, or because he possessed factual information unknown to others, but, rather, because he had developed a new position, a historical perspective, which saw
society developing in the coherent way that we now take for
granted when we refer to "historical development." This
perspective enabled him to ask new questions of the experience and records open to all. Thus, Vico was convinced that
"at the cost of the persistent research of all of [his] literary
life," he had developed a "new critical art which had
hitherto been lacking." [46] It was his conviction that this new
critical art of "etymological analysis" of the poetic material
in the fables would give the historian a "true narration" of
the people, their social organization, and science. The necessary consequence of this new approach to what man has
created is summarized in the "axiom" which states: "Doc-
trines must take their beginning from [the beginning] of the
matters of which they treat." [47] This axiom states the
methodological consequences of Vico's whole understanding of the origin and development of the "poetic characters," and includes by implication Vico's conviction of both
the possibility and the necessity of coming to understand
previous historical events. Hence this axiom is the key
methodological principle of *The New Science*.[48] In this
axiom and all that it implies we see these essential outlines
of the modern historical consciousness: History is the study
by man of what man has created; concrete historical formulations, and above all language formulations, are indis-
pensable to the historian's quest; no traditions or authorities

are self-validating, but all must be traced back to their source; and the critical historical method is not only a distinctive form of knowledge, but also the "obviously true way" of arriving at the knowledge of man and the world which he has created. Even the philosophers "have failed by half" in not taking account of history in their inquiries. In summary, in the whole realm of man and what he has created there is nothing which is foreign to history, for indeed, reality is historical in nature.

SUMMARY AND EVALUATION

This concludes our description of the general outlines of Vico's understanding of man and of history, a description in which we have had to omit many prominent details. Negatively, Vico devoted his life to opposing and correcting the mathematical model of knowledge advocated by the increasingly powerful Cartesian philosophy of his day as being the normative mode of all knowledge. He did this by pointing out, on the one hand, the "fictitious" or "game" quality of the clear and distinct ideas of mathematics; and, on the other hand, by stressing (and overstressing) the "opaque" quality of the descriptive, quantitative knowledge which arises out of the natural sciences. Mathematical and scientific knowledge does not take account, he insisted, of the specifically humane qualities of man: his goals, hopes, motives, decisions, loves, fears—all that goes to make up history. In making his protest he was the first within the modern context to draw the now familiar distinction between the "two cultures": that of the natural sciences and that of the human sciences. In making this passionate, lifelong protest against the rationalism of Descartes, he is a significant forerunner of Romanticism, Existentialism, and contemporary investigations of the function of myth.

Positively, Vico's greatness lies in his being the first modern thinker to be thoroughly and self-consciously aware of history as a distinctive form of knowledge, and to give a theoretical basis for such knowledge. He asserted, as we have seen, that in addition to the commonly recognized forms of knowledge, there is self-knowledge; that this self-knowledge is manifested in all that man has created in history, and especially language and myth; that we may apprehend what other selves have created in history by means of analogy with our own experience; and that this self-knowledge which comes through the study of what man has created in history is, while admittedly lacking the clarity and simplicity of the arbitrary "fictions" of mathematics, "superior" to scientific knowledge because in the study of history we are studying our own creations, and therefore we may know their cause, purpose, and goal. Or, more simply, in the natural sciences we are only spectators; but in history we are creating participants, and truth is most assuredly derived from the study of what we have ourselves created. *Verum et factum convertuntur* ("The true and the made are convertible"). This theory is, of course, not *totally* new. Nothing is. There are significant points at which Vico and the biblical point of view are obviously at one, and the most fundamental one is their common basic conviction that reality is historical in nature. Again, there is an even more obvious parallel, if that is possible, between Vico and Augustine's *Confessions*, with its concern for the dynamic, developing self, and the knowledge of self which may come through the retrospective analysis of its actions. Nevertheless, when all of this has been said, Vico is original in at least three respects. First, he becomes highly self-conscious and relatively systematic about what is usually implicit only in Scripture and in such writers as Augustine. Second, he defines the realm of history for the modern world by means of his critique of Cartesianism and in his exposition of history as a distinctive mode of human knowledge. Third, he draws attention to the critical role of language and myth in the historian's endeavor to gain access to the past.

EXCURSUS

In the following chapters we will be returning to Vico's ideas because we believe that they are pertinent to the discussion of the relationship of history, language, and theology in our own day. Before proceeding, therefore, it is appropriate that we deal briefly with the question of the lack in Vico's *New Science* of any traditional sense of God's transcendence. According to Vico, "the fabric of human society is created by man out of nothing, and every detail of this fabric is therefore a human *factum*, eminently knowable to the human mind as such." [49] Does the exclusion of the concept of transcendence from *The New Science* render Vico's account of historical experience essentially incompatible with the Christian faith?

Vico the man, it is worth mentioning, was a devout Roman Catholic; and there is no convincing evidence to suggest that this devoutness was feigned.[50] As far as the ideas expressed in *The New Science* are concerned, the situation is ambiguous; and consequently Vico's work has been read in different ways.[51] Thus, we find in Vico, on the one hand, a powerful sense of man's sinfulness, his involvement in community, the rejection of any rationalistic reduction and dehumanization of man, and the conviction that history is guided by "divine providence." Here Vico's continuity with the Christian faith is obvious. On the other hand, in Vico the presence of the divine within history is conceived of very strictly in terms of immanence. Vico indicates that he recognizes the problem here by specifically excluding biblical history from his purview.[52] He then indirectly admits, as his book proceeds, the inadequacy of this dichotomy by alluding to biblical events as examples of historical principles arising out of the study of "Gentile," i.e., nonbiblical, history.[53] This exclusion of transcendence, in the sense of any divine interruption of historical processes, is, of course, entirely consistent with his fundamental position: History is the critical study of what *man* has made. In taking this position, Vico was once again foreshadowing a development which would extend far beyond his time; in this case, the slowly growing and often painful realization that in historical explanation we may not set man aside in order to posit a divine intervention—even when the history in question is that which forms the content of the New Testament. History is the study of what man has made, and the attempt to establish a special hermeneutic for a special kind of history—holy history—has come to be recognized increasingly for the unsatisfactory solution which Vico two centuries earlier seems to have sensed that it was, and which we know that it is. The general result has been, seemingly, an increasingly strong sense of the immanence of God, and a radically diminished sense of God's transcendence.

This development, however, needs to be understood and stated in a somewhat more incisive way; and when we do so, the relevance of Vico to this development will become clear. A better way of expressing what has taken place is to say that we have arrived at an understanding of God's transcendence in which it is seen more fully than before that transcendence cannot be separated from immanence, and, indeed, in which transcendence points to a dimension (whether "depth" or "height" or whatever) of immanence, and says of it: This is a more than human and historical possibility, even though it is absolutely associated with humanity and history. Thus the assertion that the Christ existed before the foundation of the world—certainly a transcendental statement—can only be understood as pointing to a dimension of our human and historical experience of God's immanence in Jesus of Nazareth. In short, the distinction between transcendence and immanence has often been overdrawn. It is helpful to remember, as Kenneth Hamilton has recently reminded us, that not only are the assertions of God's transcendence and the assertion of his immanence *both* faith assertions, but they are *equally* faith assertions.[54] One does not require more or less faith than the other; rather, they are two aspects of one faith experience, one arising *with* the other. This, of course, is just the understanding at which the Church arrived in its christological discussions in the ecumenical councils, in which it came to be agreed that our encounter with Jesus' divinity arises *with* our experience of his humanity, and the attempt to separate the one from the other cannot be tolerated. Thus Gerhard Ebeling can write: "That salvation is to be expected from God alone and that it is to be expected from the word alone, and therefore it is both wholly of God and wholly of man—these statements are not paradoxes or oddities." [55] Leslie Dewart assumes the same position, but takes it further, when he advances the suggestion that "Christian theism may in the future conceive God as a historical presence, indeed as History, yet a history that would destroy neither human freedom nor God's reality precisely because such a God would not be [in the Hellenic mode of thinking] eternal." [56]

We will return to this matter in the following chapters, but at this point we would want to advance the judgment in regard to Vico, that even in his exclusion of God's transcendental activity from *The New Science*, Vico has not really placed himself outside the Christian understanding of experience. Moreover, even those modern historians who have gone beyond Vico and have omitted all discussion of God's immanence, have, nevertheless, a fundamental connection with the biblical point of view because modern historical categories are fundamentally biblical categories.

3

Toward a Post-Cartesian View of History: The Quest of the Historical Jesus and the Theology of Rudolf Bultmann

The problems with which Vico wrestled in *The New Science* are still unresolved problems of history and theology today: What is the character of historical knowledge? How do we arrive at such knowledge? What may we expect of it? And so on. It is the purpose of this chapter to examine how these and related problems were handled in the two theological movements that lead from the arising of the modern historical consciousness in Vico's day to the discussions of the relationship of history and theology in our own day. These two movements are the so-called quest of the historical Jesus, and the existentialist theology exemplified in the work of Rudolf Bultmann.

Our procedure will be to comment briefly upon certain outstanding characteristics of the quest of the historical Jesus; and then to examine in much greater detail Bultmann's handling of the problem of the relationship of history and theology. The justification for this procedure is, first, that a review of the historical-Jesus movement has been made too frequently to need repetition here;[1] second, that a considerable degree of scholarly consensus exists as to the significance of the movement; and third, because some of the most fundamental presuppositions of the quest of the historical Jesus reappear in the work of Bultmann. In contrast, Bultmann's work remains problematic in the extreme, and its largely unresolved issues continue to be the starting point of current theological discussions concerning the relationship of history and theology.

THE CONTEXT OF THE QUEST OF THE HISTORICAL JESUS

In the century following Vico, a number of the problems and ideas with which he had dealt became common property; for example, the idea that man is the creator of his own world, that the realm of history is a distinct source of knowledge with important consequences for all areas of life, that authorities and traditions must be approached critically, and so on. This revolutionary development was diffuse in its origin and growth, however, and was not dependent upon the work of Vico to any significant extent.[2] This absence of any significant Vichian influence explains in part why, during this period and until relatively recently, certain of the ideas so important to Vico failed to manifest themselves generally. Primary among these was the crucial distinction drawn by Vico between, on the one hand, the clear and distinct knowledge which is appropriate to such disciplines as mathematics, and, on the other hand, the form of knowledge which is appropriate to history. Closely related to this, and scarcely less important, was Vico's recognition of the fundamental relationship between language and history. In the absence of these most critical insights as to the nature of history, the attempt was made to use the dominant Cartesian or scientific model of knowledge in the field of historical inquiry. The ideal was to ascertain, clearly and distinctly, the objective *facts,* that which *really* happened.[3] (If such an ideal was entirely foreign to Vico's thinking, it is nevertheless true that certain of the attitudes developed by him were thoroughly suited to encouraging this ideal; for example, that man is the creator of his world, the necessity for the careful examination of the origin of what man has made, skepticism toward authorities, and so on.) The endeavor, extending over two centuries and to some extent into the present day, to achieve this ideal has been characterized by Van A. Harvey as an "almost Promethean will-to-truth." [4] The appropriate response to this effort must be, in spite of its limitations, one of gratitude. It established, once-and-for-all, in the slow, thoroughgoing way necessary in any major cultural change, that the uncritical acceptance of evidence, the claims to finality, the polemic, the "exemplary tale," etc., have no place in the process of historical inquiry. In more positive terms, this development (whatever its deficiencies as to depth) was the assertion that "the nature of things is nothing but their coming into being at certain times and in certain fashions." It is true that the excesses of this development were many; but these excesses, as in any major cultural change, must be seen against the background of the institutional and cultural conservativism which had to be overcome.

THE QUEST OF THE HISTORICAL JESUS

The particular manifestation of this new ideal of history which concerns us most directly here is the bringing of this modern historical consciousness to bear upon biblical history, and particularly upon the life of Jesus of Nazareth. In the so-called quest of the historical Jesus, all the characteristics of the critical, historical study of Scripture are raised, and raised in an especially acute form. The period in which this "quest" took place may conveniently be set as beginning with David Friedrich Strauss's *Life of Jesus* (1835), and ending with Albert Schweitzer's *The Quest of the Historical Jesus* (1906). The presuppositions and goals of those who engaged in this first quest were essentially no different from the presuppositions and goals of other his-

torians of the period. Consequently, the quest of the historical Jesus shared the strengths and weaknesses which, as we
have discussed, marked historical inquiry generally in this
period. It is to the abiding credit of the liberal theology of
the nineteenth century, and probably the characteristic for
which it will be remembered in the textbooks of the future,
"that it exposed itself to the inevitable encounter with the
historical-critical method and the all-embracing historical
understanding, thus showing the theology of its time the
way to freedom and truth." [5] Liberal theology, in Bultmann's judgment, "gained its character essentially through
the predominance of an interest in history." [6] Of course, we
understand this much more fully now than at the time it
took place. The explicit aim of liberal theology was to
cease to ground the Christian faith in metaphysics and
dogmatic speculation, and to ground it anew upon the solid
foundation of clear historical fact. The center of the enterprise was to be the "historical Jesus," that is, Jesus insofar
as he could be known through critical-historical inquiry.[7]
In other words, "historical" was a polemic term directed
against all metaphysical and dogmatic speculation, and the
term "historical Jesus" meant in effect the "true, real
Jesus." [8] As D. M. Baillie has remarked, "In the modern
age of criticism and questioning, the rediscovery of the
human historical personality came as a new realization of
the historical content of the dogmas: men found in the Gospel story a real human personality which constrained them
to say, with the Church and in the Holy Spirit, 'Jesus is
Lord'. . . ." [9] It does not take a great deal of imagination
to see even now the attractiveness of this program, especially when it is placed against the theological conservatism
and the exegetical obscurantism which was the context
within which liberal theology had to find its way.

One aspect of this original quest of the historical Jesus,
the critical interpretation of myth, calls for special attention,
because of its intrinsic importance to that quest and because

of the importance of myth in our own inquiry. Although Vico had developed a critical and sophisticated interpretation of myth (from which biblical material was carefully excluded) a century earlier, it was with the publication of Strauss's *Life of Jesus* that the problem of the relation of myth to the Christian faith became a paramount issue. In Norman Perrin's judgment, the long-term effectiveness of Strauss's work has not been in terms of his Hegelian approach to history and to Christology, but "in terms of a growth of understanding of the gospels as myth and saga." [10] Strauss's criticism was directed not only against the "Supernaturalists"; but also against the rationalist approach to Scripture which, after "explaining" the miraculous incursions into nature and history, left the substance of Scripture intact. In contrast to both of these approaches, Strauss and many who followed him argued that Scripture as a whole reflects an understanding of reality alien to our own, namely, a mythological understanding of reality which sees human and natural events as being under the direct influence of supernatural beings of all kinds.[11]

Thus the problem was set. It was to be explored extensively by various disciplines, including the new discipline of the history of religions. As a result of the cumulative historical study and reflection of these various disciplines upon the phenomenon of myth, it became increasingly clearer in the century following Strauss that these stories did not refer to the "objective" reality which seemed to be their purported subject. As this became clearer, the question of what it was that myths were actually concerned with became more and more insistent. As in the study of the life of Jesus, so here too in regard to myth, a Cartesian approach to experience was increasingly seen to be of very limited use.

From a Cartesian viewpoint, the historical phenomenon of myths has to be understood in the limited way which is still so familiar, that is, as being the primitive attempt at science and technology (aetiological and fertility myths),

as expressions of community or tribal solidarity (the Mesopotamian city gods), as the expression of such psychological
states as fear, wonder, pride, and so on. In other words,
myths were primitive or ignorant or misleading attempts to
speak in terms of the stories of the gods of what were in
fact such "objective" realities as natural phenomena, community organization, psychological states, or even religious
experience. In this way, so it was and is asserted, myth can
be totally explained.

This rejection of myth, so prominent a part of Western
civilization from the Enlightenment until the present day,
is in an important sense a continuation of the struggle, in
both the Old and the New Israel, against the pagan gods of
the Near East and of Europe. The Enlightenment did not
have to give the term "myth" the highly negative connotation
which it still has today, for the term had already acquired
that significance during the centuries-long struggle of the
Church against the myths of the pagan gods.[12] That struggle
had been carried on through the truth and power manifested
in Jesus of Nazareth, who lived and died and rose again,
and who will come again in the last days. This was no
myth. Rather, as the Church through the centuries had
asserted both by argument and by force, it was the "true
story" that overcomes all the darkness of myth! With the
rise of the historical, critical method, however, the worm
turns; the "true story" which had triumphed over the pagan
myths, can itself be understood as myth. The strictures
applied to the pagans can, in part at least, be applied to
the gospel. If one accepts the clarity and distinctness of
ideas as being the criterion of truth, then having moved
from many gods to one, it seems only reasonable to eliminate God altogether. In this situation it is also reasonable,
having eliminated the demons of nature by means of the
Christian faith, to go on to eliminate the notion that nature
is created by God and is consequently suitable to be used
by his Spirit as a means of grace.

These, then, are the very real contributions, both positive

and negative, of liberal theology's "quest of the historical
Jesus," including its attempt to deal with the phenomenon
of myth. The implications of these contributions are only
becoming fully evident today. That this quest is generally
agreed to have been a failure only attests, although in a
way which the liberals did not understand, to one of the
major theses of their program: namely, the historically
conditioned and provisional nature of the Church's statements about Jesus. For, as Schweitzer pointed out in his
The Quest of the Historical Jesus, the picture of Jesus which
emerged was largely determined by the presuppositions of
the men who produced the endless stream of "portraits of
Jesus" in the nineteenth century. The presuppositions were,
in general, those of nineteenth-century humanism. Heinz
Zahrnt refers to these presuppositions as those of an "ideal-
istic historical pantheism," and characterizes them in words
which are applicable not only to their manifestation in the
nineteenth-century lives of Jesus, but also in many sermons
still preached to Christian congregations Sunday by Sunday.

It was thought that the divine goal of the historical process was
the gradual triumph of the powers of the True, the Good and
the Beautiful, which were understood to permeate history after
the analogy of natural forces. Mankind is making its way step
by step from a state of nature to civilization. The individual man
shares in this struggle by making himself open to these spiritual
powers and hence from his state of nature developing a free
personality. Every now and then individuals appear in history
who carry within themselves these supernatural powers to an
extraordinary degree. One of these bearers of revelation, perhaps the greatest and most supreme, was Jesus of Nazareth.[13]

What were thought to have been historically objective
lives of Jesus, came to be seen to be dependent upon the
standpoint of the authors; and none more so than the mystic,
apocalyptic interpretation of the life of Jesus presented by
Schweitzer himself in *The Quest of the Historical Jesus*.

Although the publication of Schweitzer's book in 1906 may fairly be taken as marking the end of the liberal quest for the historical Jesus, the quest came to an end not because of that book, but, as James M. Robinson has pointed out, because of the growing realization on all sides at the turn of the century that the documents of the New Testament are not objective, positivistic documents but, rather, reflections of various aspects of the life of the primitive Church.[14] The difficulty with the liberal's quest was the same difficulty which marked historical writing generally in the nineteenth and early twentieth centuries, and the same difficulty to which Vico had tried to speak: the misconception of historical knowledge in terms of clear and distinct ideas, demonstrable to all, and convincing to anyone with the willingness and skill to review the evidence. In other words, the Cartesian model of knowledge, so appropriate to the natural sciences, was taken into the field of history, where it would not work.

That this model would not work is attested to not only by the failure of the whole movement to find the historical-critical Jesus, but also by the continual smuggling into the various lives of Jesus of the very unclear and indistinct ideas of nineteenth-century humanism. This smuggling also attests, however, to the correct, albeit largely unrecognized, perception by the liberals of the issues involved. That is to say, the exalted status which the liberal theologians desired to ascribe to Jesus could not be derived from the New Testament record, at least when that record was understood in terms of the ideals of nineteenth-century historical inquiry. (Ironically, the desire to ascribe this status to Jesus was the result of the influence of the traditional Christology which the liberals wished to destroy.[15]) Therefore it was necessary that some substitute basis for Jesus' status be supplied. The result was that the "para-Christology" of nineteenth-century humanism, flying the flag of "objective historical facts," was smuggled in to supply this basis. When, increasingly, this situation came to be recognized for what it was—more than a decade before Schweitzer's book of 1906, Martin Kähler had pointed out in a more profound but less provocative way than Schweitzer, this fundamental fault in the quest of the historical Jesus[16]—then the whole enterprise collapsed. The mistake had not been in directing attention to the Jesus of history but, rather, in the use of a restricted notion of history which made it inevitable that the categories of nineteenth-century idealism would be imposed upon the historical, biblical material.[17] A further development of the quest of the historical Jesus, and of the relationship between history and theology, would have to wait upon a new, less restricted understanding of history. No one man contributed more to this development than Rudolf Bultmann. Therefore, it is to certain relevant aspects of his work that we now turn.

RUDOLF BULTMANN

The work of Rudolf Bultmann, whose voice has dominated the discussion of the relationship of history and theology for a generation, constitutes a major step forward in reapprehending the significance of history for Christian faith and theology. Bultmann's contribution lies in his general, although not complete, movement away from the Cartesian approach to history which dominated and distorted the nineteenth-century quest of the historical Jesus; and a general, although again not complete, movement toward an appreciation and use of history which is in accord both with the biblical understanding of reality as being historical in nature, and with the modern formulations of that understanding as developed by Vico and others. Bultmann has made this contribution primarily in terms of, first, his theory of the nature of historical understanding in which his frequently reiterated distinction between "historical" (*historisch*) and "historic" (*geschichtlich*) plays a large part; and second, and less successfully, in terms of his understanding of myth. In both of these areas the insights and categories of existential thought have been of critical importance. Bultmann's ideas in these two interrelated areas are fundamental to his total theological endeavor.

Before entering into an examination of these two areas, however, the volume and intensity of the controversy which has centered around Bultmann calls for special comment, and for an explanation of our own selective approach to it. In part this controversy has taken on its present dimensions due to Bultmann's occasional lack of precision. The almost journalistic tone of certain portions of his influential essay, "New Testament and Mythology," is a particularly vivid case in point.[18] A more significant reason for Bultmann's ability to attract controversy, however, is the fact that he has focused for us the central theological problem (or complex of problems) of our time. This problem may be indicated in various ways: the relation of history and theology, the problem of revelation, the nature of the relationship between God and the world, the quality of responsible language about God, hermeneutics. Whichever approach one takes, one keeps coming back to the underlying and interrelated issues of language, myth, and history. It is to just these issues that Bultmann has consistently directed the attention of the Church. While general agreement has been reached that we cannot be content with Bultmann's handling of these issues, we have, nevertheless, not been able to develop a definitive criticism of Bultmann's position, much less a widely accepted alternative.[19] We find ourselves in this situation for the very basic reason that contemporary theology has made only partial and tentative decisions about how it is going to handle the issues of language, myth, and history that Bultmann has done so much to force upon our attention.

The complexity and intensity of this controversy necessitates our own selective approach to it. We will engage the discussion at those points where it directly affects the controlling theme of this book: the interpretation of history and its relation to theology. Since history, as we have seen, cannot be discussed apart from the phenomena of language and myth, we will also want to consider what Bultmann and his critics have to say about those matters. Thus, our approach will take us into what we understand to be the heart of the controversy around Bultmann, but we do not pretend to a comprehensive review of the issues and the discussion which they have provoked. We turn first, then, to Bultmann's distinction between *Historie* and *Geschichte*.

The Unity of Historie and Geschichte

The distinction which Bultmann makes between objective history (*Historie*) and existential history (*Geschichte*) is, in the terms of our own discussion, the means whereby he moves away from a Cartesian or positivist approach to history. Therefore, in spite of the fact that the matter has often been reviewed by Bultmann's critics, it will be advisable to state this distinction once again. It is worth noting here that we have not found it necessary to make this distinction before, either in our discussion of the biblical foundation of historical thought, or in its modern development by Vico. The distinction, which seems to have been introduced into theological discussion by Martin Kähler around 1892,[20] does serve the purpose of drawing our attention to two dimensions of history. The distinction may also be, as we shall see, as misleading as it is helpful.

When Bultmann speaks of history (*Historie*) and the historical (*historisch*), he is referring to history in its "objective" rather than its existential aspect; that which may be established by critical, historical research; that which moves in the realm of I-It.[21] In H. Richard Niebuhr's terms, history here is "outer" rather than "inner" history; history which gives factual information about the world.[22] History in the sense of *Geschichte*, on the other hand, is history which is nonobjectifying; "inner" history which moves in the realm of I-Thou, evoking decision and commitment from the participants. Bultmann frequently characterizes *Geschichte* as *existentiell,* that is, as pertaining to the understanding which the individual has of his own unique, personal existence.[23] Concretely, the execution of Jesus of Nazareth in Jerusalem, around A.D. 30 is a matter of *Historie;* that this death is a means of reconciliation between God and man, moves in the realm of *Geschichte.*[24]

In making this distinction between *Historie* and *Geschichte,* it is not Bultmann's intention to make the positivist's separation between "fact" and "interpretation" which characteristically marred the historical and biblical studies of the nineteenth century. "*Geschichte* and *Historie . . .* are closely connected and yet distinguishable." [25] Indeed, the connection is so close that one cannot be understood in isolation from the other.

This *existentiell* relation to history is the fundamental presupposition for understanding history. This does not mean that the understanding of history is a "subjective" one in the sense that it depends on the individual pleasure of the historian and thereby loses all objective significance. On the contrary, it means that history *precisely in its objective content can only be understood by a subject who is* existentiell *moved and alive.* It means that, for historical understanding, the schema of subject and object that has validity for natural science is invalid.[26]

The understanding of history reflected in this statement makes a substantial contribution toward showing us the way out of the impasse created by positivist historiography and liberal theology in its quest of that will-o'-the-wisp, the "clear and distinct idea." In the discussion which follows we will assume the unity (*not the equation*) of *Historie* and *Geschichte.* Consequently, unless we indicate otherwise, our use of the term "history" may be understood as "*Historie-Geschichte.*" We believe that our argument will show the validity of this assumption.

The degree of clarity which Bultmann has achieved re-

garding the relationship of *Historie* and *Geschichte* emerges
in his essay, "Is Exegesis without Presuppositions Possible?"
There he points out that while the historian must strive
constantly to eliminate from his work the false presuppositions constituted by bias, "the one presupposition that cannot be dismissed is *the historical method of interrogating
the text*." [27] It is in this sense that there is no such thing as
presuppositionless historical inquiry.

What is the content of the presupposition condensed into
that short phrase, "the historical method"? Bultmann points
to two areas. First:

The historical method includes the presupposition that history
is a unity in the sense of a closed continuum of effects in which
individual events are connected by the succession of cause and
effect. This does not mean . . . that there are no free decisions
of men whose actions determine the course of historical happenings. . . . [but that] All decisions and all deeds have their
causes and consequences; and the historical method presupposes
that it is possible in principle to exhibit these and their connection and thus to understand the whole, historical process as a
closed unity.[28]

Bultmann's statement cuts two ways, destroying two
abstractions: that of positivism and that of "supernaturalism." On the one hand, the positivist's abstraction of a
rigidly closed historical process is replaced by the position
that, while history is a closed continuum of cause and effect,
man's freedom is one of the causes affecting history. The
historical method *presupposes* as much, for it understands
man as he who, standing in the tension of promise and fulfillment, is the creator of history, who can know that which
he has created (cf. Chapter 2). On the other hand, Bultmann's statement denies the abstraction of "Supernaturalists" and others that man or nature may be moved directly
and unambiguously by divine intervention; or that man has
an unconditioned freedom which enables him to interject

causes or actions into the historical process which are not the product of historically determinable factors. This position of the "Supernaturalist" is just as much an abstraction as that of the positivist. Those who accept history as being the "true story" about life, have no experience of either. Nor may we conveniently forget this when we come to the study of Scripture, for there is no special biblical hermeneutic which permits us at that point to put aside the criteria of critical historiography.[29]

We should note here, since it is relevant to our later discussion of Bultmann's understanding of myth, that while the "supernatural" is eliminated, *that* which man creates in his historically conditioned freedom is not eliminated. Thus the way is provided for the free, human creativity so essential to all historical experience. Moreover, this characteristic of history (*Historie-Geschichte*) is the basis for affirming the validity of that particular form of free human creativity which comes into being in man's faith assertions. Such assertions cannot be proved by critical historiography (*Historie*), but they do not violate or rend the historical (*historisch*) apprehension of the world. Indeed, as we sought to establish in the preceding chapter, history, including the *historisch* element, is dependent upon the faith perception (or mythic affirmation) that reality is historical in nature. This is the presupposition of critical, historical inquiry. Of course, the result of the use of a presupposition cannot prove the validity of that presupposition. What can be established, however, is the *usefulness* of the presupposition for understanding experience; and certainly the fruits of the use of the presupposition of the historical nature of reality do establish its usefulness.[30] We will return to this as our discussion of Bultmann develops.

The second group of presuppositions implicit in the phrase, "the historical method," has to do with what Bultmann calls a "life-relation" between the historian and the subject matter which he wishes to understand.[31] By this he means that if an event is to be grasped historically, then it must be understood; and if it is to be understood it must be translated into language and ideas with which we have a life-relationship. This translation is the task of historical science. "If we speak of translation, however, then the hermeneutical problem at once presents itself. To translate means to make understandable, and this in turn presupposes an understanding." [32] And later: "One cannot understand the decisions of persons who act in history if one does not understand man and his possibilities for action." [33]

At this point, however, Bultmann is not sufficiently clear. An understanding, or "pre-understanding" as he sometimes refers to it, is presupposed. But which understanding of man and the world is presupposed? Not any understanding will do; not that of, say, Mesopotamian civilization, or that of Mahayana Buddhism. Rather, here again, precisely a historical understanding of man and the world is presupposed by historical inquiry. Therefore, when Bultmann says, "In short, historical understanding presupposes an understanding of the subject matter of history itself and of the men who act in history," [34] it is worthwhile emphasizing that this "understanding of the subject matter of history itself" is no neutral or objective deposit possessed by all men, but is in fact available only through the exercise of historical understanding. Its verification is not a matter of experiment and the establishing of clear and distinct ideas but, rather, an Anselmic movement of experience and affirmation in which what can only be called "faith" seeks to understand itself in terms of its own categories. "To understand history is possible only for one who does not stand over against it as a neutral, non-participating spectator, but himself stands in history and shares in responsibility for it." [35] One shares in this responsibility because one is responsive to the demand and necessity for decision inherent in it; and because one is committed to the historical enterprise of discovering and exercising the creatorhood of historical man in relation

to the past, present, and future. In this situation one is within the hermeneutical circle; the study of history is clearly a
case of faith in search of understanding. It is, however,
faith in *search* of understanding. While it is true that the
relationship and approach to the subject under investigation
is presupposed to be historical in nature, this pre-understanding "may be a quite naïve and unreflective one, and in
comprehension or interpretation it can be brought into the
conscious mind and clarified . . . . it may be deepened
and enriched, modified and corrected by understanding the
text" [36] or other phenomenon under investigation. In this
way we see that the pre-understanding of reality as historical is the way God has given to the Old and the New
Israel to be attentive to the world, to recognize and to
create new forms of meaning in the world. History (*Historie-Geschichte*) is a structure of grace which enables
man to be for the world.

It is important to emphasize the difference between this
position and the position of radical relativism, which Van
Harvey refers to as "Hard Perspectivism." [37] Harvey maintains, and we would agree, that "Hard Perspectivism" attempts unsuccessfully to assert that all historical judgments
are relative to the perspective of the historian, and that
therefore no one historical judgment may claim to be more
valid than another. In this situation, counsel is confused as
"fact"; and interpretation, *Historie* and *Geschichte,* become
indistinguishable. In our judgment, the position which we
have developed in this area is in accord with Harvey's,
namely, that some judgments about the course of past
events are more entitled to credence than others;[38] and that
we are not the prisoners of our preconceptions because
"human beings possess sufficient possibilities of self-tran-
scendence to arrive at unpleasant truths, that is, judgments
which run counter to their treasured hopes and desires." [39]
Our pre-understanding *does* determine our relationship to
the historical object, and is essential for the formulation of

the questions which we address to it; but this precludes
neither the deepening or radical reformulation of our
questions, nor the exercise of our freedom in the grasping
of new possibilities for human understanding in the encounter with the events of history.

Hard Perspectivism makes its mistake, if we may elaborate upon Harvey's analysis, when it applies its perspective
at the wrong level. Instead of illegitimately arguing for the
subjectivity of *every historical judgment,* and thereby calling
into question the legitimacy of any such judgment, it could
legitimately apply its strictures against the historical understanding of reality *as a whole.* That is, one should and must
accept the "subjective" character of history in the sense that
it rests finally upon a faith affirmation, and that no criterion
or methodology exists to establish its merits as over against
the various affirmations of the ahistorical nature of reality.
At this level the strictures of Hard Perspectivism, appropriately modified, do apply (although, admittedly, the
polemical purposes of Hard Perspectivism are not very
clearly served by this extension of their argument). The
recognition that this is so delivers us from the arrogant
affirmation that our own perspective, our own "true story"
of history, encompasses all truth without remainder.

In the light of these considerations, let us ask again in
what sense is it that Bultmann maintains that history in its
aspect as *Historie* is concerned with that which is "objective," "critical," "factual," and so on? The answer can
only be that history in its *historisch* aspect *is* objective, given
the presuppositions with which it operates. This is no mere
token objectivity; rather, it is one form, the historical (*historisch-geschichtlich*) form, of the only kind of objectivity
which is possible: that which arises out of disciplined inquiry based upon fundamental presuppositions and an appropriate methodology. Bultmann has helped us to understand that history does not have the clear and distinct ideas
characteristic of scientific objectivity, but it does have its

own appropriate presuppositions, goals, and methodology, including rules of evidence. The claims of historians are verifiable within the community of historians; and when the historian participates in this community and its presuppositions, including especially for Bultmann the element of demand and decision which is so much a part of historical existence, then objective historical knowledge is possible. "In this sense the most subjective interpretation of history is at the same time the most objective. Only the historian who is excited by his own historical existence will be able to hear the claim of history." [40] In arriving at this understanding of history, we have moved decisively beyond the Cartesian limitations of nineteenth-century historical and biblical inquiry.

The Dynamics and Significance of Historical Decision

Thus far we have presented Bultmann's understanding of history in its related but distinguishable aspects as *Historie* and *Geschichte;* we have explored the implications of the unity of these two aspects, together with the implications this has for positivism and "supernaturalism"; and, finally, we have examined in some detail the role of pre-understanding in this approach to history, together with its significance for the much-debated issue of historical objectivity and subjectivity. With this preparation we may now go on to state relatively concisely Bultmann's existential understanding of how historical events and judgments are continually reapprehended, and the significance which these have for man's "existence" or "being" or, more historically perhaps, simply "life."

Bultmann proposes, instead of the Cartesian quest for the facts as they actually are, that we let our approach to historical existence and knowledge be guided by the concept of the "moment" in which historical events are again and again interpreted and reapprehended. This interpretation and reapprehension, since it arises "out of the claim of the

now," cannot be understood in terms of a detached act of
the intellect; but, rather, in terms of a moment of decision
in which the intellect participates, but in which the will is
"the determining factor." [41] Bultmann has this existentially
conceived moment of decision bear the greatest possible
weight: It is the individual "I" who stands in this moment
of risk and decision; the moment grows out of my historical
situation, "out of the claim of the now, out of the problem
that is given in the now." [42] The moment is one of encounter
and suffering leading to decision and self-knowledge as
"the yield of the past is gathered in and the meaning of the
future is chosen." [43] This moment of decision is the responsibility of men, for it is not in some causal connection of
events, but "In this responsibility, as responsibility over
against the past as well as over against the future, the unity
of history is grounded." [44] Thus man is engaged in a continuing act of creation as again and again he stands in the
present moment of decision: questioning, reinterpreting,
translating, and reapprehending the past with the result
that there emerges new self-knowledge (new possibilities
of being) for "the *I*, as an ever-growing and becoming, an
ever-increasing, improving or degenerating *I*." [45] We will
resist commenting upon the incredible dynamic which becomes explicit here, and which, with all its creative and
demonic possibilities, has been so much a part of the historical spirit of Western civilization. Instead, we wish to go
on to examine in turn the two halves, "the yield of the past"
and "the meaning of the future," which are united in the
"now" of historical decision. Our examination will show
that Bultmann's grasp of the second half of this unity is
much stronger than his apprehension of the first.

    What Bultmann means in this context by the phrase,
"the meaning of the future," is pointed to in a provocative
way in his frequent contention that the future of a historical
event belongs to that event. [46] This characteristic of historical event is acknowledged, however inarticulately, in the

common recognition that every generation must write its own history and its own theology. Bultmann, in exploring this matter in greater depth, turns, like Vico, to poetry in order to explicate his position. In poetry, as in narrative and historical texts generally, there is laid open to sympathetic understanding "the *possibilities of man's being*." [47] This is the "truth" which the creation of poetry intends, namely truth in the "radical sense" of "the laying bare of human being." [48] When it is expressed in this way it becomes evident, as Bultmann intends that it should, that the truth which man has made, whether in its specifically poetic or more generally historical forms, cannot be apprehended as an object or deposit or fact lying in the past. Rather, truth, and specifically historical truth, can only be recognized when it is understood as laying bare the possibilities of human being *"that belong specifically to the one who understands"*;[49] and this means, by implication, those possibilities which yield meaning for my living in the future which lies beyond the present "now" of historical decision. Demythologization, to which we shall turn later, is obviously the attempt to do just this.

Hence, the historian is sensitive to the specifically humane and personal qualities of the phenomena which he studies;[50] he recognizes that the report from the past is about something which man has created, and about which he as a man is called again and again to evaluation and decision concerning its significance for himself.[51] In Buber's words, "only [in this way] can man, confident in his soul, build again and again, in a special conception of space, dwellings for God and dwellings of men . . . and shape the very community of men." [52] Therefore, insists Bultmann, there can be no appeal to historical events as objective deposits in the past which may be used to "prove" historical judgments. Historical judgments by their nature cannot yield clear and distinct ideas, proofs, coercive arguments, final statements, and so on. The common idea that they should

rests upon the underlying assumption, which we have
shown to be mistaken, that it is possible to completely
separate objective history (*Historie*) from existential history
(*Geschichte*), and then to argue from one to the other.
This procedure is literally incomprehensible, since the underlying assumption—that we may proceed from *Historie*
to *Geschichte*—is something of which we have no experience. Rather, according to Bultmann, within the context of the understanding of reality as historical, and with
the help of historical methodology which is organically
related to it, historical events are reapprehended as laying
bare possibilities for our future being, and as calling for
decision by our own being, to choose that future. It is in
this sense that Bultmann affirms: "To be historical means
to live from the future." [53]

This affirmation of the ongoing, future-oriented quality
of historical experience is all quite abstract, however, until
it is joined to the "yield of the past." Living "from the future," by itself, has the abstractness and formlessness of the
Protestant principle and Protestantism generally, of new
ages of the spirit and of apocalypticism. It is the "yield of
the past"—Catholic substance, if you will—which comple-
ments this abstractness and renders the situation genuinely
historical. We have seen how Bultmann realizes this in his
description—again abstract—of the necessity of the union
of past and future which takes place in the moment of
decision.

In concrete terms, what is this "yield of the past" that is
joined to the "meaning of the future" in the moment of decision? It is that which man has created in the past (for
example, the Sistine Chapel, Boswell's *Life of Johnson,* the
battle of Gettysburg) apprehended *as history* (or, as we
would prefer, *apprehended within the context of the myth
of history*).[54] In order for this to take place, however, not
only must we apprehend the event as opening up possibilities for our present and future being, but we must also have
the freedom to actualize these possibilities.

Bultmann denies, however, that man of himself possesses the freedom necessary for the historical apprehension of experience. "Christian faith," affirms Bultmann, "believes that man does not have the freedom which is presupposed for historical decisions." [55] The reason for this lack of freedom is that one is "coined by his past," and hence not free from one's past experience, illusions, mistakes, victories—not free from oneself and from the often secret desire to stay as one is. In this situation one strives to control the future by preserving the past, or better, certain favorable elements out of the past: power, wealth, the law, the eternal verities. Here the past is called by such names as "fate," "karma," and the "principalities and powers." Here, overwhelmed by the past, the possibility of creatively disposing over past and future history (in distinction from withdrawing from it, or submerging oneself in it) cannot be conceived, and history is impossible. The possession of such power of disposition presupposes that one knows in some degree the goal or meaning toward which history is directed, and that one possesses the freedom to move toward it. The Greek historians, by way of contrast, did "not raise the question of meaning in history, and consequently a philosophy of history did not arise in Greece." [56]

Since man cannot achieve freedom, it must be given to him as a gift; and this gift is given to him "by the revelation of the grace of God in Jesus Christ." [57] It is this historical (*historisch-geschichtlich*) event, Jesus the Christ, who is the meaning-giving, eschatological event which, in the moment of decision, I recognize as being yielded by the past, as living into the future, and as being present in the "now" of my decision. Through this manifestation of love in Jesus the Christ, and through our own responsive love to the preaching of God's act, we are freed from ourselves and from our past. We now understand that the meaning and goal of existence, "the eschatological event," has appeared within history; and that we ourselves are to participate in the meaning insofar as again and again we affirm that meaning for our-

selves. In Bultmann's terminology—of which the creative
possibilities for preaching generally have never been adequately realized—we now understand our freedom and
genuine selfhood as coming to us as "a gift by the future." [58]
"To be historical means to live from the future"; [59] we
understand ourselves "as future." From this position the past
no longer overwhelms us; the demon of fate, like the demons
of nature, has been overcome. Now we may legitimately
and creatively dispose of the meaning of past and future in
the present of historical existence.

It is in this way that Bultmann understands Jesus the
Christ to be the foundation and criterion of all genuinely
historical existence.* Jesus the Christ, presented through
preaching and present in faith, is the paradigmatic historical
event in which the "yield of the past" is joined to the "meaning of the future." Apart from this original relational event,
the realization of meaning which comes to expression in it,
and the tensions between past promise and future fulfillment which it establishes, the understanding of reality as
historical would not be possible.[60] In our own terms, it is
this event which gives expression to the myth of history.

The Fallacy of the False Disjunction

Now, it must be admitted that the firm relationship in
Bultmann's thought between Christian faith and history represents an emphasis or interpretation upon our part of one

* We do not intend to enter into a discussion of Bultmann's view of
the *specifically Jewish* contribution to the historical understanding of
reality. This decision is due partly to Bultmann's limited discussion of
the subject (cf. Bultmann, *Essays*, pp. 182–208; cf. also Rudolf Bultmann, *Primitive Christianity in Its Contemporary Setting*, trans.
R. H. Fuller (New York: Meridian Books, 1956), pp. 59ff.), and partly
due to the complexity of the subject. Bultmann would maintain at least
that the radical understanding of history reaches its fulfillment in Jesus
the Christ. We would agree with this judgment, although our line of
argument would not take exactly the same course as Bultmann's does
(cf. Chapter I, *supra*). For a discussion of certain difficulties in Bultmann's understanding of Judaism, see Samuel Sandmel, "Bultmann on
Judaism," in *The Theology of Rudolf Bultmann*, pp. 211–220.

aspect of Bultmann's understanding of history. We have documented this aspect of Bultmann's thought, and this documentation could be readily extended. Nevertheless, Bultmann is, in fact, ambiguous about the relationship between Christian faith and history. Perhaps the closest that he comes to being unambiguous in this matter is his statement:

But there can be no doubt that the *radical* understanding of the historicity of man has appeared in Christianity, the way being prepared in the Old Testament. This is proved by the fact that real autobiography arose for the first time within Christianity. From this origin the understanding of the human being as historical became effective in the West, and it remained vivid even when it was divorced from Christian faith.[61]

We are not told what a nonradical "understanding of the historicity of man" might be, and it does not seem to be very useful to speculate upon this.

However, over against Bultmann's positive statements as to the relationship between Christian faith and history, including the statement which we have just quoted, we must set those statements in which faith and history are separated. In these statements *Historie* and *Geschichte* cease to be "closely connected and yet distinguishable" elements or aspects in historical consciousness, and instead threaten to lose their connection. Thus Bultmann writes: "Christ is everything that is asserted of him in so far as he is the Eschatological Event. But he is not this in such a way that it would be expressible in terms of a world event." [62] Or again: "the crucified one is not at all proclaimed in the New Testament in such a way that the meaning of the cross would be disclosed from his historical life as reproduced by historical research." [63] Or, yet again, and even more radically and disconcertingly, when with approval he quotes Erich Frank: " '. . . to the Christians the advent of Christ was not an event in that temporal process which we mean by history today.' " [64]

It is in these and similar passages that Bultmann, in spite
of everything else he has said, tends to reassert the separation between event and interpretation, or, in R. G. Collingwood's terminology, to take up the Fallacy of the False Disjunction. When this disjunction is present, there arises once
again the whole problematic question of the continuity
between event and interpretation, including specifically the
question as to the continuity between the historical Jesus
and the Christ who is affirmed by Christian faith. It is just
upon the problem of this continuity that the criticism of so
many of Bultmann's critics comes to a focus. Now, Schubert
Ogden argues—in opposition to Robinson, Macquarrie and
other critics—that Bultmann has always acknowledged the
continuity between the historical Jesus and the Christ of
faith.[65] We believe that Ogden's argument is successful.
(Bultmann has always *acknowledged* this continuity, even
if he has maintained it imperfectly.) It is noteworthy, however, that the strength and clarity characteristic of Ogden's
exposition of Bultmann's thought becomes weak at just this
point. This weakness is due to an inadequacy in Bultmann's
thought, an inadequacy which Ogden accepts in part, the
inadequacy of the False Disjunction. It is the presence of
this inadequacy which explains why so many critics, occu-
pying such varied positions, have difficulty in understanding
Bultmann. Let us look into this more closely.

Ogden's exposition of Bultmann's thought in this area is
weak, first, because he argues with Bultmann that we cannot
now "understand the meaning of the Cross *in the same direct and unmediated way in which it was grasped by the first
disciples*—namely, as an event in their own lives set in the
context of their personal experience of Jesus' life and
work." [66] This and similar statements in Ogden and Bultmann seem to reflect the point of view that history, at least
as it takes place, gives rise to the assurance which comes
with clear and distinct (*"direct and unmediated"*) ideas.
This is not true of our own experience, and the New Testa-

ment indicates that the "possibilities for being" manifested in Jesus of Nazareth were no less difficult for the disciples than for us.

A second and much more important weakness in Bultmann's position, and again one which Ogden supports, is the limited significance which Bultmann attaches to what may be known about Jesus as a result of critical historical inquiry. Ogden, after arguing at length that Bultmann *does* believe it to be possible to arrive at critical historical knowledge of Jesus, and that there is continuity between this historical Jesus and the Christ of faith, goes on to concede indirectly much of what Bultmann's critics are contending. Ogden writes:

Bultmann holds, however, that while such a process [of critical historical reconstruction] is possible, it is hardly necessary. For, "the crucified one is not at all proclaimed in the New Testament in such a way that the meaning of the cross would be disclosed from his historical life as reproduced by historical research." [67]

Presumably this means that while critical historical knowledge of Jesus is possible, it is at best largely irrelevant— "hardly necessary." (Later in the book, Ogden, with a "consistency" which Bultmann lacks, drives Bultmann's position to what he considers to be the necessary conclusion: ". . . faith in Christ, can be realized apart from faith in Jesus or in the specific proclamation of the church." [68]) This is just what Bultmann's critics are objecting to, and we would judge that their objection is essentially a correct one. None of the critics mentioned wishes to argue that faith in Christ can be proved or simply "read off," clearly and distinctly, from the historical record. History does not provide that kind of knowledge. At the same time, however, faith does not arise *in separation* from the historical record and the event to which it testifies. If such a separation or disjunction is asserted, and Bultmann does *tend* to make this assertion, then history in the full sense which we have described in this book, is not taken seriously; that which man—in this case, Jesus—has created in history is not taken seriously. The "yield of the past" is reduced to an abstract "thatness" which is then, quite consistently, eliminated by those who wish to develop this perspective to its ultimate conclusion. In terms of our own analysis, this introduction of the False Disjunction assumes that critical historical knowledge has an independent status, which in fact it does not possess; and it also falsifies the dynamics of historical knowledge by obscuring the intimate relationship between existential, historical interpretation in the "now" of decision, and the content of the past in relation to which the decision is made. Whenever this disjunction appears, it manifests itself in the most dubious ways, as, for example, when Bultmann affirms that faith must be held apart from history in its *historisch* aspect because God "can only be believed upon in defiance of all outward appearance," and that this "is in fact a perfect parallel to St. Paul's and Luther's doctrine of justification by faith alone apart from the works of the Law." [69] Bultmann's position, in other words, is that history (*Historie*), like sin and good works, looks to the past; while eschatological history looks to and lives from the future. But this is just the disjunction which, we have maintained, violates the nature of historical existence and knowledge.

Another way of pointing out the falseness of this disjunction is to call attention to the experience of each of us, that we seldom live exclusively at either end of the polarity which is called, variously, "past and future," "outer history and inner history," "I-It and I-Thou," and so on. This is not to deny that these polarities are extremely useful for purposes of analysis; however, it is to deny that all or even most of our experience can be located exclusively at one pole or the other.[70] Between these two poles much significant living, much significant exploration of the possibilities of being, takes place. This means, for example, that critical historical work on the life of Jesus need not be, and seldom if ever is, exclusively oriented to the past. Rather, it is, even in its more technical phases, normally invested to some extent by the promise of the future. This is only another way of expressing what we have argued at length: that the experience of reality as historical, and the critical historical methodology which has developed out of it, is itself a structure of grace which has grown out of and is dependent upon the view of God, man, and the world found in Scripture. Consequently, there is more room *in the life of faith* for the past and for the critical (if you will, "objective") study of the past than Bultmann allows. Consequently, we would want to agree with Father Cahill's nicely balanced appreciation and criticism of Bultmann in this matter:

Assuredly the distinction between faith and theological understanding will not always and in every instance be clear. . . . The existentialist, biblical approach common to Bultmann and his followers has done well to restore the intersubjective, faith-emphasis of Scripture which could be underemphasized by a more speculative approach. . . . Stress on *geschichtlich* as opposed to *historisch,* the concrete as opposed to the abstract, the intersubjective and personal as opposed to the speculative and impersonal, is necessary if theology is to retain its biblical and religious orientation. On the other hand, if theology is to be both relevant and intellectually respectable, one cannot wish to exclude the *historisch,* the abstract, the speculative and the impersonal.[71]

We would want to go further, and emphasize what we have asserted before, namely, that the *historisch* cannot be separated from faith, and that the greatest abstraction of all is to make false disjunction between *Historie* and *Geschichte.* Whenever Bultmann makes this disjunction he fails to carry through the insight of our nineteenth-century liberal heritage that critical historical inquiry and Christian faith have the closest possible relationship; that Christian faith, even in its most eschatological aspects, has no need to fear or be

aloof from critical history; and that Christian faith can take
the yield of the past, including all of its ambiguities, with
complete seriousness, giving thanks to God for what he has
enabled man to create in the past.

Myth and Its Relation to History

Bultmann's approach to history and his approach to myth
are intimately related. In spite of the fact that the nature and
function of myth have been the principal focus of attention
in the controversy around Bultmann, we have not entered
directly into that area up to now. The primary reason for
our taking this course is our belief that the results of the
examination of Bultmann's view of history will throw new
light upon the unresolved, but now somewhat dusty, controversy surrounding Bultmann's program of demythologization. Because the closest relationship exists between Bultmann's approach to history and his approach to myth, the
same difficulties emerge in both areas.

In Bultmann's definition of myth, myth and *Historie*
possess significant common characteristics. Objectification,
which, as we have seen, is the primary characteristic of
Historie, according to Bultmann, is also regarded by him as
being the primary characteristic of myth. He writes:

Myth is spoken of here in the sense in which it is understood
by research in the history of religions. Mythology is that manner
of representation in which the unworldly and divine [*das Un-
weltlich, Göttliche*] appears as the worldly and human—or, in
short, in which the transcendent appears as the immanent [*das
Jenseitige als Diesseitiges*]. Thus, in the mythological manner of
representation, God's transcendence is thought of as spatial dis-
tance.[72]

Thus myth, like *Historie*, falls within the subject-object cor-
relation fundamental to all acts of abstract, objective knowledge. Further, myth, like *Historie*, is existentially useless,
and hence useless for faith; for just because of myth objectification, it cannot speak to man in his struggle to under-

stand himself in the world. "The invisibility of God excludes every myth which tries to make him and his acts visible. . . . God withdraws himself from the objective view." [73] Hence, the attempt to rely upon myth is like the attempt to rely upon the "facts" established by *Historie;* and both attempts may be paralleled to the attempt to establish and secure one's faith by means of good works. Myth, so understood, is "this-worldly" in the worst sense; it represents the dead hand of the past, of the "old man," upon us.

In Ogden's judgment, the "clue to the whole constructive thrust of his [Bultmann's] work is his insight" that it is this objectifying nature of mythic thought which renders it inadequate to speak of "the ultimate existential ground and end of man's being as a historical person." [74] The New Testament itself calls for our deliverance from the inadequacy of myth in that it calls for our deliverance from the powers of this world,[75] and this deliverance is already starting to be worked out in the New Testament itself in the theology of Paul and of the Fourth Gospel.[76]

These are, briefly, the essential outlines of Bultmann's understanding of myth.[77] We would like to make several statements by way of appreciation and support. First, we would agree with Ogden that Bultmann's definition of myth is clearly stated and consistently held.[78] One may disagree with the definition, but that is another matter. Second, insofar as myth as Bultmann understands it is present in Scripture and in theology, then we must maintain with Bultmann "not only that we can dispense with it, but that it is essential to do so." [79] The basis for our agreement with Bultmann in his rejection of myth (as he defines it) is that myth, so understood, is just as much of an abstraction as is *Historie* when it is understood as being completely objectivized, in isolation from *Geschichte,* and neutral in its relation to life. Myth and history in this sense really do not exist at all; that is, it is impossible for living, creative mythic or historical thought to take place within such a conceptual scheme. It is, of course, true that some persons *believe* themselves to

be operating within such a framework, but that is again
another matter.[80] Third, in fairness to Bultmann, and in the
interest of clarity of discussion in a troubled area, we need
to be clear as to what is *not* excluded under his definition of
myth. The Christ-occurrence, to take the most central example, is not intrinsically a mythical occurrence.[81] This may
sound like an amazing assertion to many within and, even
more, without the Christian faith. In Bultmann's terms,
however, this is quite consistent and unremarkable. Bultmann would say that in order to be genuinely understood,
the Christ-occurrence must be interpreted, as it clearly
always has been, in existential terms: the possibility for
authentic being offered by God through Christ; the risk inherent in decision and commitment; faithfulness in response
to Christ's address; and so on. Once this has been done, the
objective-fact-in-the-past quality of the Christ-occurrence is
dissolved, and *by definition* it is no longer mythic. Hence
Bultmann may assert roundly: "I deny that the Christian
faith is for man intrinsically mythological." [82] The practical
theological consequence of the way in which Bultmann thus
delineates the problem is that although he rejects "myth," he
is left with a quite rich and useful theological language and
conceptualization: namely, the traditional Christian language and conceptualization, existentially modified.

Turning to the negative side of our appreciation of Bultmann's concept of myth and demythologization, the main
point which we want to make is that while his concept is
clear and consistent, it is artificially and unnecessarily restricted. This results in the continual creation of confusion
in theological discussion. In *Christ without Myth,* Ogden, in
his defense of Bultmann's use of myth, repeatedly must ad-
monish the critics to remember the definition of myth which
Bultmann has proposed.[83] Ogden is technically correct, but
the critics' confusion is not entirely unjustified, since Bultmann's definition of myth is so artificially restricted that it
is really unworkable. Hence, it is not just the obtuseness of

the many critics which necessitates Ogden's repeated admonition: "Think." Or, to qualify our statement slightly, Bultmann's definition is workable only if one makes the assumption or judgment that myth in Bultmann's sense really exists. Myth, in Bultmann's objectivized sense does not exist except as a secondary abstraction for the same reasons (as we have argued, and will argue further) that an isolated, objective *Historie* does not exist except as a secondary abstraction. Positively, insofar as the secondary abstractions of myth and *Historie* are used, they continue to be dependent for their "existential capital" upon the primary and fuller understanding found, respectively, in genuine myth as we have defined it in Chapter 1, and history (*Historie-Geschichte*). (Parenthetically, the objections to this "narrowness" in Bultmann's definition cannot be met adequately, although Ogden attempts to do this, by stating that they are "irrelevant," since Bultmann has explicitly defined myth in a narrow way![84]) It is for these reasons that we would argue that the introduction of this very restricted and thereby confusing understanding of myth obstructs as much as it helps in achieving the central objectives in Bultmann's theological program.[85]

Now Bultmann is fully aware of myth in its broader sense, the sense in which we have been using it throughout this book; and he speaks of it as the "real purpose" of myth.

The real purpose of myth is not to present an objective picture of the world as it is, but to express man's understanding of himself in the world in which he lives. . . . Myth speaks of the power or the powers which man *supposes* he experiences as the ground and limit of his world and of his own activity and suffering. . . . Myth is also an expression of man's awareness that he is not lord of his own being.[86]

This real purpose of myth, however, is "impeded and obscured" by the objective terms in which it is expressed. Man only *supposes* that the powers acting upon him are those spoken of by myth. Accordingly, the service which existential interpretation performs for faith is to free this real meaning from the imagery in which it is enshrined. Specifically, in regard to the New Testament, "faith ought not to be tied down to the imagery of New Testament mythology." [87] This does not mean, Bultmann has consistently maintained, that myth is to be eliminated—except perhaps "here and there"! That was the mistake of the older liberal theologians. Rather, the mythology of the New Testament is to be interpreted in order that man may "discover whether the New Testament offers [him] an understanding of himself which will challenge him to a genuine existential decision." [88]

Does Bultmann really believe that myth in its origin or continued usage has the objectified character which he describes in his definition of myth? Apparently so. In "A Reply to the Theses of J. Schniewind," Bultmann elaborates his understanding of myth, and in the course of doing so speaks of "mythology in its original sense." [89] It is just this original sense, he maintains, which it is essential to eliminate. In making this proposal Bultmann assumes, anachronistically, that the ancient peoples who created myths thought of themselves and their subject matter in an objectifying way. Surely it is not necessary to document the findings of research into primitive and not-so-primitive religions, that just the opposite is the case. Or can we appeal to our own experience in reading of the fire god, Agni; of Gilgamesh; of Krishna; of the exodus narrative; and so on? Here is mythology, certainly, in the sense that the transcendent appears and is described in terms of the things of this world; but, apart from the objectification necessary in *any speaking,* where is the sense of objectification, of subject over against object, of proof? What we do find is the strongest sense of the presence of the immanence of the transcendent, and of our identification with it. There moves throughout all of these and other such myths the still powerful sense—even for us—of existential involvement. Surely these myths are performing just what Bultmann maintains is the "real purpose" of myth, which "is not to present an objective picture of the world as it is, but to express man's understanding of himself in the world in which he lives." [90]

What is at work here leading Bultmann into such an odd position is the same fallacy of the False Disjunction which we noted in his distinction between *Historie* and *Geschichte;* except here it is present in a more extreme form. We saw how Bultmann describes at length the significant interrelationship of *Historie* and *Geschichte,* although he finally fails to carry through on this insight. However, Bultmann's understanding of the relationship between, on the one hand, myth and, on the other hand, the existential interpretation or "real purpose" of myth, is even less satisfactory—it is existentially rather thin. It is true that the relationship is sufficiently strong that myth is not to be abolished (except "here and there"), but nevertheless myth tends to be that which "enshrines" real meaning, that to which real meaning is "tied down." Moreover, while *Historie* is, as we have seen, *incomplete* by itself, myth *falsifies* or distorts because its forms are those in which man "supposes" he experiences the world around him. In other words, while Bultmann's False Disjunction interferes both in regard to history and to myth with full attentiveness to what man has created, the disjunction and consequent inattentiveness in regard to myth is more radical. Here we are close to a "facts *plus* interpretation" position.

We can see a further similarity between Bultmann's treatment of myth and his treatment of history by asking of him how the Christian is to find or understand the meaning which he once "supposed" he understood and possessed in mythic terms? His answer to this question is that, as a result of the existential analysis of the traditional mythic material, we are to reappropriate the Christian faith in eschatological terms. Whether in regard to *Historie* or myth, it is Jesus

Christ who effects this for us. Hence, once again, we may say, "*Jesus Christ is the eschatological event,* the action of God by which God has set an end to the old world." [91]

What we see in Bultmann's thought, then, is a substituting of the "historical-eschatological" for the "mythical." In this substitution "historical-eschatological" fulfills exactly the same function as traditionally has been fulfilled by the mythical: namely, the expression of man's understanding of himself in God's world, and his creative engagement with God's world. The "mythical moment" experienced in, say, preaching or the Eucharist, is replaced by the "historical-eschatological moment." This is what has taken place in Bultmann's theology rather than the rejection of the mythical in any significant sense. This is, in effect, a remythologization. This remythologization has been worked out basically in terms of the myth of history; and, as such, it is, in spite of the reservations which we have indicated, to be welcomed as a powerful statement of the Christian faith for our time. Bultmann's program, so much better in its overall results than in *some* of its theoretical pronouncements which are disjunctive and reductionist in nature, is a manifestation of what Paul Ricoeur speaks of as "the second immediacy that we seek and the second naïveté that we await [and which] are no longer accessible to us anywhere else than in a hermeneutics; we can believe only by interpreting." [92] This process of interpretation leading to restoration (of which Bultmann's remythologization is a part) seeks "to go beyond criticism by means of . . . a criticism that is no longer reductive but restorative." [93] Our epoch holds in reserve both the possibility of "emptying language by radically formalizing it [as in disjunctive approaches to history and myth] and the possibility of filling it anew by reminding itself of the fullest meanings, the most pregnant ones, the ones which are most bound by the presence of the sacred to man." [94] It is this process which Bultmann and his followers have done so much to begin, and which certain contemporary theologians concerned with the relationship of language to history and theology are doing so much to further. This second group is articulating a position that will preserve the very substantial contribution which both the "quest of the historical Jesus" and Bultmann have, respectively, made to our understanding of history and its relation to theology, but which is going on to overcome the False Disjunction found in that work. The overcoming of this disjunction permits, we are convinced, closer attention to the substance of what man has created in past history.

4

Toward an Erotics of History:
Language and History

Susan Sontag, in her essay "Against Interpretation," maintains that "In place of a hermeneutics we need an erotics of art." [1] While recognizing the correctness of Nietzsche's dictum, "There are no facts, only interpretations," Sontag nevertheless maintains that Western civilization's *preoccupation* with analysis, interpretation, "true meaning," etc., has come to be a stifling approach to experience, at least in the realm of literature. "The interpreter says, Look, don't you see that X is really—or, really means—A? That Y is really B? That Z is really C?" [2] Crucial to the rationalization of this procedure is the "odd vision" in which something we have learned to call "form" is separated from something we have learned to call "content." The former is accessory ("hardly necessary," in Bultmann's terms) and the latter is essential; and the process of interpretation is to discern the content behind the form. [3] Demythologization exactly!

As a liberating alternative to "interpretation," Sontag calls for a greater attentiveness to form in art; for the development of a *descriptive,* rather than an analytical and prescriptive, vocabulary for forms; and for a "really accurate, sharp, loving description of the appearance of a work of art." [4] The goal of this erotics of art is "transparence."

"Transparence means experiencing the luminousness of the thing in itself, of things being what they are." [5] An erotics of art will seek this transparence of experience by showing us how our experience *is what it is,* even *that it is what it is,* rather than to show *what it means.*" [6]

Although Sontag is speaking as a literary critic, we believe that the position which she takes is equally applicable to the area of history and theology. Hence, we would make bold to modify her aphorism, and to say: "In place of a hermeneutics, we need an erotics of history." Sontag's concerns and our own come together because both have to do with the function of language in the apprehending, recording, and reapprehending of human experience. We believe that the way forward in the effort to appreciate what is taking place in history and theology lies in a new and closer attention to the role of language in these areas.

The role of language has never been far from the center of our attention in this book, and in our discussions of Buber and Vico, respectively, this concern has received our direct attention. It is central to Buber's position, as we have seen, that "I become through my relation to the *Thou*; as I become *I,* I say *Thou.*" [7] "The *Thou* meets me through grace . . . But my speaking of the primary word [*Thou*] to it is an act of my being, is indeed *the* act of my being." [8] Such language is not something apart from man and his thinking, not an abbreviation or arbitrary symbolization of his thought; rather: "When a primary word is spoken the speaker *enters the word and takes his stand in it,*" [9] "for in actuality speech does not abide in man, but man takes his stand in speech and talks from there." [10] Hence, "All real living is meeting," [11] and life cannot be conceived of apart from language. In this "language-meeting," man "receives not a specific 'content,' " not a clear and distinct idea, "but a Presence, a Presence as power" [12] marked by the "whole fulness of real mutual action," and the "inexpressible confirmation of meaning" which desires expression in this

life and in relation to this world.[13] We believe that this
may fairly be said to be one expression of an "erotics" of
language and experience.

In our examination of Vico we discovered a position
which, while expressed in its own unique terminology, is
remarkably similar to Buber's. Vico affirms that the most
important thing which man creates is language. The "first
men" (yes, well . . .) "were poets who spoke in poetic
characters," and the discovery of this "primary operation
of the human mind" is the "master key of this Science," i.e.,
of history.[14] These "poetic characters"—words, myth, language—are most significantly characterized as "true narrations" which had and have "natural relations to the ideas
they wished to express." [15] At its most fundamental level
language is, in our contemporary terminology, intrinsically
related to that which it signifies; or, language is performatory in nature. Moreover, the specifically historical way in
which Vico understands this theory of language emerges
clearly when he asserts, "The nature of things [*verum*] is
nothing but its coming into being at certain times and in
certain fashions [*factum*]." [16] What is it that comes into
being at certain times and in certain fashions? Fundamentally, it is the language which man makes. Moreover,
"minds are formed by the character of language, not
language by the minds of those who speak it." [17] There
is no "eternal idea" or "revelation" or "fact" or "clear
and distinct idea," etc., which somehow stands behind the
language, and for which language is a sometimes more,
sometimes less adequate pointer or abbreviation. (Or, if
there is such a "hidden reality," we have no way of knowing
what it is.) Rather, the historical reality arises with the
language which testifies to it; and that language has a "natural" or intrinsic relation to the historical reality.

Building upon this foundation, it is our purpose to show
how, by means of a new responsiveness to language, an
erotics of history is being constructed in contemporary

theology. It is somewhat ironic that this is being done most significantly under the banner of the "new hermeneutic." However, the "newness" of the new hermeneutic lies, as we shall see, in an "erotic" approach to language, the hermeneutic process, and history.

BACKGROUND TO THE NEW HERMENEUTIC

What is meant by the new hermeneutic will emerge as our discussion progresses, but a preliminary definition at this point will be useful. In simplest terms, the new hermeneutic is the attempt to arrive at a theory and practice of the interpretation of texts which stresses a particular approach to language and to history. The approach to language may be characterized in a preliminary way by Gerhard Ebeling's statement: *"The primary phenomenon in the realm of understanding is not understanding OF language, but understanding THROUGH language."* [18] Robinson comments upon this aspect of the new hermeneutic: ". . . the assumption characteristic of the new hermeneutic [is] that the language pointing to the subject matter is not simply in need of interpretation, but is already itself an initial interpretation of that subject matter." [19] Or, in terms of our previous discussion, one does not try to reach an understanding of language by "penetrating" to the thought which supposedly lies "behind" language, but one "takes his stand in speech and talks from there."

The particular approach to history characteristic of the new hermeneutic may, for the purposes of our preliminary description here, be indicated by saying that it is the concept of history which we have been discussing throughout this book in terms of the myth of history.[20] Hans-Georg Gadamer reflects the position of the new hermeneutic when he maintains that "In reality history does not belong to us but we to it." [21] Paraphrasing Buber, we could say that, from the perspective of the new hermeneutic, "Man takes his stand in history and talks from there." [22] This substitution of "history" for "speech" in Buber's statement is possible because, when history and speech (language) are approached as we have approached them here, they stand in the closest possible relationship. More specifically, we take our stand in the myth of history, but this myth is shaped in us by our very language, and is inconceivable apart from that language, i.e., inconceivable apart from the particular significance which is bodied forth in such words as "exodus," "covenant," "the Christ," "hope," "the new," "reign of God," and so on. It is in *this* sense that to take our stand in history is the equivalent of taking our stand in language.

The new hermeneutic begins, to a very significant extent, with the thought of Martin Heidegger;[23] and both have striking similarities with the work of Vico. Vico and Heidegger stand in the same fundamental intellectual tradition, e.g., in their opposition to objectifying thought as the primary means of apprehending reality; in their insistence upon the primacy of man's self-knowledge; in their conviction that language is the key to such knowledge; and even in the preoccupation with etymological analysis which marks the work of both men.

Vico believed that his contemporaries had gone astray in their approach to the reality of history, and, as we have seen, his corrective for this situation was to invite his contemporaries to examine their experience in a new way; namely, through the examination of primitive experience of the "first men" who were poets, and "truthful by nature." In the same vein, Heidegger, who believes that the traditional approaches to philosophy have gone astray, invites us to look at philosophy in a new way, which is also an older way that has been forgotten.[24] In advocating this approach, Heidegger, like Vico, is in revolt against the intellectual tradition that we have characterized variously as "objectifying," oriented to "control," "Cartesian," etc.[25] This tradition, says Heidegger, is "that of *calculating* which in this day and age everywhere tugs at our thinking";[26] and this is not only manifested in the natural sciences and technology, where we would expect it, but has captured our metaphysical thinking as well. Heidegger's contention is that this preoccupation with the abstracting kind of thought involved in calculating, differentiating, controlling, etc. has made us forgetful of a more primordial kind of thought which is essential to our humanity; and which is, moreover, the ground out of which our abstractions arise. In other words, in a movement of thought very close to Vico's, the clear and distinct idea is recognized as being useful, but also as simply not being adequate to plumb the totality of human experience. For this another kind of thinking and language are necessary. Consequently, Heidegger's whole work is an effort to "shed a little light on the path . . . which is 'backtracking' from metaphysics into the essence of metaphysics, from oblivion of difference as such [i.e., the clear and distinct idea]" [27] into the fateful issue which we no longer understand. That issue is Being, and the thought and language which is receptive to Being. Heidegger repeatedly directs us to the mystery expressed in Leibniz's question: "Why are there entities at all, and not just nothing?" Heidegger's effort to deal with this question is conceived of in terms of man, and of what man has made in response to the call of Being. Robinson expresses this nicely:

Man takes place as man when he is addressed by being. Man is the place where being clears so that one catches sight of it and exclaims "There!" This is the meaning the later Heidegger attributes to his designation of man as "being-there," *Da-sein*. Thus both Heideggerian terms for man, existence and *Dasein*, envisage man as the place where being opens up and reveals itself.[28]

Being opens up or is "unveiled" in man in the process of originative thinking (*unfangliche Denken*). This thinking stands in contrast at every point with the abstracting, calculating, and controlling thinking of the Cartesian tradition. Originative thinking, on the one hand, "carries out" man's nature and, on the other hand, is the form in which the action of Being upon man manifests itself.[29] Man is constituted, Being is revealed. Originative thinking stands at the center of Heidegger's philosophical effort: "It expresses the rapport between the existent and the things-that-are that achieves what Heidegger calls the *Wahrung der Wahrheit,* i.e., Being's own self-essentialization. Originative thinking builds truth and protects what is gained in the process." [30] Originative thinking is, in Buber's terms, the "inexpressible confirmation of meaning."

How, concretely, does this meaning express itself? As in Vico and Buber, so in Heidegger: in language. "Speech does not abide in man, but man takes his stand in speech, and talks from there." [31] Or, in Heidegger's famous formula: "Language is the House of Being." In his earlier work, Heidegger leaves open the question as to whether all originative thinking is not at the same time a speaking or "poetizing." This hesitancy in his earlier work to bring thinking and speaking into the closest possible union, Heidegger would ascribe to its still "too philosophical" nature.[32] In his later, postwar works this hesitancy is overcome. Language, in the broad sense which would include music and the visual arts, is the act through which Being itself comes home in language.[33] In this forming of the "House of Being," Heidegger, in striking parallel to Vico, "regards the poet as mankind's true priest. It is he who names the gods, who speaks forth the world of meaning that being addresses to him . . ." [34] In his essay on Anaximander, Heidegger writes:

Thinking, however, is poetizing (*Dichten*), and indeed not just a kind of poetizing (*Dichtung*) in the sense of poetry or song. The thinking of Being is the fundamental manner of poetizing. In thinking thus considered, language comes to be language primordially, i.e., in its essence. Thinking pronounces the *Dictare* of the Truth of Being. Thinking is the fundamental (*ursprüngliche*) *Dictare*. Thinking is the root-poetry (*Urdichtung*) from which all poesy follows, also all that is practical in art, insofar as art comes in its activity into the region of language. All poetizing in this very wide sense, and also in the narrow sense of poesy, is in its ground a thinking.[35]

The thinker *thinks* Being in terms of language; the poet-priest names the holy, the gods, in language. (The "holy," for Heidegger, may be understood in some such sense as the supreme fulfillment of man and of things.[36]) This thinking and naming are two correlative aspects of the same reality and activity. "The poet and the thinker share the responsibility of 'bringing Being to house' in forging language." [37] In *this* thinking and naming, Being is unveiled or comes to expression in language; and the neglect of *this* thinking and naming in the West has led to a correlative forgetfulness of being and forgetfulness of the holy.

Although we cannot enter into all the details of Heidegger's analysis of language, two other dimensions of this analysis must be mentioned because of their direct pertinence to our concerns. The first of these dimensions is Heidegger's insistence that originative thinking and language never take place in a vacuum, but always in relation both to things and to history. Heidegger sets forth the place of things in the thinking and speaking of Being in terms of the "square," the fourfold unity which binds what we call "thing." This square is described somewhat enigmatically but meaningfully as being composed of (1) the Earth, the constructing supporter and fructifier; (2) the Heaven, the Sun's course and the path of the moon, the times of the year and the blue depth of the ether; (3) the Divinities (*Goettlichen*), the fleeting messengers of the Divinity (*Gottheit*) through whose hidden rule appears God in his essence; and (4) the Mortals, men, for whom the prospect of death,

of Nothing, protects the realization of being. "If we pro-
nounce 'mortals' " (or "Earth" or "Heaven" or "Divinities"), says Heidegger, "then we think of the other three
without the unity of the four"; that is, we have entered into
abstraction and subject-object analysis, and are forgetful
of Being. In contrast, to see a "thing" on the fullness of its
four aspects is to see that "thing" essentially, in the dimension of Being.[38] (This description of an encounter with a
"thing" seems to us to be close to a description of the ways
things are perceived in the ancient canticle, the *Benedicite*;
as it is also, in Buber's terms, close to "Thou-saying" to the
created world.[39]) Although Heidegger's statement is de-
liberately obscure, what is clear is the serious taking account
of things in the world, and the seeing of them as integral to
the perception of meaning. This is inevitable once a high
evaluation has been placed upon language, for language, as
conceived of by Heidegger, is a naming of things in which
the "name" and the "thing" cannot be separated, since it is
in the very naming that the being of the "thing" comes into
view—although never completely, for the mystery of being
always remains. Similarly, language is itself a "thing,"
sounds and symbols made by man (the *factum,* in Vico's
terms) and organically related to that which language
names.

If "things" hold an important place in Heidegger's
scheme, so does history, and for very similar reasons. If
being comes to itself in language, and if language is the
House of Being, then there must be attentiveness to the past,
and specifically to the meaning which has been created in
the past through language. Consequently, essential or originative thinking is not only concerned with the contemporary
and ongoing realization of Being, but must also of its very
nature, "look to the past, reawaken it, and protect it." [40]
The receptiveness to Being must include a receptiveness to
Being manifested in past language. It is just upon the basis
of a lack of sensitivity to language and the attendant lack

of receptiveness to Being, that Heidegger attacks the "meta-physical" tradition extending from Plato through Descartes to the present. This "metaphysical" tradition has made us insensitive and "unloving" in regard to the past, unable to experience the "luminousness of the thing in itself, of things being what they are," [41] and presents us with the false option of either passively accepting the past as a "factual" descrip-tion of what took place (e.g., historical positivism and Fundamentalism), or of rejecting the past in the spirit of radical historical skepticism.

The reawakening and protecting of the past is only pos-sible because man in the present (*Da-sein*) brings certain capacities to bear in experiencing what comes out of the past. In this connection it is pertinent to identify two funda-mental and closely related presuppositions of Heidegger's philosophy.

The first of these presuppositions is that man possesses and is responsible for the inherent capacity of thinking and naming which enables him to *respond* to and show forth Being. Man does not initiate and control thinking; rather, man's thought has a receptive structure which enables him to perceive and reawaken and reappropriate Being, which is presented to him in the subject matter of the present as it comes out of the past. This capacity, it is further presup-posed, may be thought of as the capacity for language: language brings the past manifestations of Being into the present, and enables us to reawaken them for the present and for the future. It is Heidegger's emphasis upon this re-ceptive quality of man's thinking and language which we consider to be the most relevant aspect of his thought for contemporary theology. We will return to this later.

The second fundamental presupposition involved here is that man possesses a criterion for distinguishing between that authentic thought which concerns Being; and the sec-ondary form of thought which does not think about Being, but which objectifies and calculates and obscures Being.

This criterion is, of course, essential or originative thinking; but "where" does this thinking come from, and what are its credentials for being the norm of thinking and existence? Heidegger, although he points to the pre-Socratic philosophers as the first known manifestation of the "letting be of Being," does not answer this question; and from his perspective, the question does not need an answer. Essential thinking is that which *is ultimate,* and for that very reason it cannot authenticate itself in terms of anything more ultimate. Essential thinking, we may say, "comes to pass." Being creates the need within man (*Da-sein*) for the thinking which answers the need of Being, namely, the thinking through which the Truth of Being is verified and protected. Man, in a thankful surrendering or sacrificing of himself to this need and the thinking which answers to it, achieves the freedom and meaning which characterizes authentic existence.[42] Langan comments that for "Heidegger the ultimate that is 'beyond man' is *Da-sein,* the Being-there [of man] among the things-that-are that is founded in the ultimate transcendence of our finite existence. . . . the 'sacrificial offering' which we must make lies in devoting our existence to the Being achieved in the wedding of the things-that-are with the temporal, [yet] transcendental horizon. This devotion, in its purity, is the end of authentic existence." [43] Being comes out of the past, addresses and is appropriated by *Dasein* in the present and for the future. This means that while the truth of Being is part of our present authentic existence, it is not at man's disposal; we never reach the point where future response to and reappropriation of Being becomes unnecessary. In this Heidegger recognizes the eschatological nature of Being. "The Being of the things-that-are gathers itself up (*legesthai, logos*) in the last moment of its destiny. . . . This *Versammlung* (gathering-together) is the eschatology of Being. Being itself is, as self-destined, eschatological." [44]

As a result of this summary of those aspects of Heidegger's thought most pertinent to our own concerns, it should be clear that Robinson is correct when he states: "In actuality Heidegger's concern with being is an effort to understand reality as historic and linguistic." [45] On a formal level, obviously, and to a substantial degree in terms of content, Heidegger's effort possesses the closest parallels with our earlier descriptions of the myth of history, and the role of language within that myth. Being is *not* God for Heidegger, but nevertheless in Heidegger's thought, the rule of God becomes, in effect, the rule of Being: an inexhaustible, hence mysterious, source of order, meaning, and hope for human existence which yields authenticity or salvation now, and which drives toward an eschatological fulfillment. The goodness and meaningfulness of God's created order proclaimed by the Christian faith is paralleled in Heidegger by the four aspects of the "squaring" of the "thing," while the responsibility of man for history is rendered in terms of *Da-sein's* perceiving, protecting, and reawakening of Being. More problematically, Heidegger's view of *Da-sein,* in conjunction with his concept of language, has suggestive parallels with the Incarnation. (The discussion in the preceding paragraph, for example, suggests the parallel.) These and other similarities lead us to agree with Helmut Franz that Heidegger derives his concept of the world from the New Testament.[46] This observation is not made in order to make Heidegger "Christian," and much less because we judge Heideggerian philosophy to be an adequate restatement of the Christian faith. It is made, rather, because we take Heidegger's analysis, whatever its deficiencies, to be a manifestation of the power of the original relational event which informs the myth of history to give rise to ever new linguistic and cultural forms; because it shows the pervasive and unitive influence of the myth of history within diverse contemporary cultural forms; and because the critical use of Heidegger's philosophy has the power to illuminate the biblical myth of history where it has been obscured by traditional linguistic formulations.

Vico and Heidegger each devoted the lonely, often eccen-

tric, labor of almost a lifetime to the attempt to deal with
one fundamental problem: for Vico this was the establishing of an epistemology and methodology suitable for the
study of history; for Heidegger it has been the attempt to
"overcome metaphysics." In both cases the attempt led to
a sustained struggle against Cartesian thought and its claim
to be the only valid approach to experience. For Vico such
thought was inadequate either for arriving at historical
knowledge, or for the perception in depth of language,
which is so much a part of the perception of history. For
Heidegger objectifying thought—that of the whole "metaphysical tradition"—is the denial of originative or essential
thinking, and an obscuring of the significance of language,
which is an indissoluble part of essential thinking. Now,
while of course Vico does not speak of language as the
House of Being, he may readily be interpreted to be saying
that language is the House of History, and by living within
this house we discover the true story of what it means to
be a historical being—*Da-sein*. In Vico's terms, originative
or essential thinking comes into language in the "poetic
characters," i.e., "certain imaginative genera (images for
the most part of animate beings, of gods or heroes . . .)." [47]
These poetic characters were produced by the "spontaneous consciousness of the earliest men" (the pre-Socratic
philosophers, presumably!), who were, by nature, both
poetic and truthful. When Vico uses "truth" in this context
he means much the same thing that Heidegger means by the
essential thinking which constitutes authentic existence.
The poet's "truth" is the constitutive act of man's human-
historical consciousness, responding to his environment,
shaping and reshaping his world. The "poetic characters"
are, in Vico's terminology, primary among all of that which
man has made (the *factum*) in history. This poetic making
corresponds, in Heidegger's terms, to those places in the past
where "Being has cleared." The study of history is the study
of this past, this *factum,* which is an integral part of the

givenness of present experience. Man's responsibility is toward this *factum,* a loving attentiveness toward it, reawakening it in the present, rendering it luminous, and so protecting the understanding of reality as historical.

Thus, our discussion of the relationship between Vico and the later Heidegger has shown that, beyond differences in terminology, they share an essentially common position in regard to the whole area of language and history. Even in regard to the most notable difference, the absence in Vico of Heidegger's awareness of the eschatological dimension of language and history, we would want to argue that this too is at least partly present by implication in Vico in terms of his insistence upon the ongoing development of language and history. Be that as it may, it is Heidegger's discussion, so thoroughly foreshadowed by Vico, of language and its implications for an erotics of history, which the new hermeneutic has picked up and developed in its relation to contemporary theology. We wish to turn now to a discussion of that development, drawing upon three of its major representatives: Heinrich Ott, Gerhard Ebeling, and Ernst Fuchs.

THE NEW HERMENEUTIC

Heinrich Ott, although his work is still largely in the programmatic stage, is the representative of the new hermeneutic whose position is most fully akin to our own. Ott, among the various theologians examined in this book, comes closest to an explicit theological exposition of the myth of history; although he does not use the term "myth" but, rather, the phrase "picture of reality." In his essay, "The Historical Jesus and the Ontology of History," Ott states: "All historical reality which we experience has a picture-like character." [48] The image of "picture" suggests a total view which is presented to us; which we interpret immediately and largely unconsciously; and which, if the

picture is authentic, carries with it immediate convincing
power of things being what they are. That this is Ott's
understanding is clear as he goes on to explain the "picture-
like character" of reality in a statement which is a perfect
functional description of myth:

. . . our experience of reality always has to do with "pictures"
and never with "facts" (we use the term "facts" consistently
in the sense of *bruta facta*). Reality always impresses itself upon
us through pictures. . . . As it impresses itself upon us it
creates within us an exposition, an interpretation, an explanation, a point of view in the widest sense, this does not even need
to be conscious. . . . In this sense Nietzsche's dictum against
positivism is justified: "There are no such things as facts, but
only interpretations." [49]

By itself, this description of the picturelike quality of
reality (and this is part of its strength) is applicable to
myth in general. It is, for example, as applicable to the
movement toward the *restitutio in integrum* of Indian philosophy, as it is to the biblical point-of-view which we discussed in Chapter 1.[50] However, as Ott develops his position,
the specifically historical way in which he sees the "picture
of reality" emerges. Reality is not something illusory, or the
private production of the individual ego. It has, rather, an
"out there" quality; it is given to us, and can be distinguished from us, for "a picture does not first arise when *we*
create a picture for ourselves. Instead, reality itself is the
first to impress itself upon us in the form of pictures. . . .
The pictures are primary; the facts [*bruta facta*] are a secondary abstraction." [51] "Pictures" are not constructions of
the historian; constructions, as well as analyses, demytho-
logizations, objective facts and so on, are secondary. Pictures, rather, "are the reality itself in the act of making itself
known." [52] Man receives the impress of reality in the form
of pictures; he experiences the luminousness of the picture
in itself, of things being what they are.[53] This implies a

fundamental personal response to, and even dialogue with, the picture. "Anything that encounters me as real is in some way significant for me." [54] The picturelike quality of historical reality which we encounter and which impresses itself upon us, and hence has significance for us, constitutes the criterion for what is "real." "Every being which exists historically, perhaps any being which exists at all, is as such significant. It is significant *as such;* that is, its significance is not only one of its many attributes, but *its significance constitutes its very being*." [55] As a result "man in the world no longer remains an inviolable subject secure in his posture and postulates." [56] Instead, we have the "true story" which, on the one hand, exalts and places responsibility upon man since it is he that receives ever new meaning as a result of his ongoing encounters with pictures of reality; but which, on the other hand, crushes man if he assumes that he is the inviolable subject who is in control of, and has the power of disposal over, what is presented to him in successive historical pictures.

It is the exploration of this historical picture of reality, Ott affirms, which will lead Christian theology into something utterly new and revolutionary, although we may not yet say exactly what this will be. The way forward, however, is pointed out to us in the work of Heidegger.[57] "The thinking of Martin Heidegger performs the inestimable service of teaching us to see in a more primal way the nature of thinking, of language, and thus of understanding." [58] This primal or essential thinking, which comes to expression in language, is based upon the receptive nature of man's thought, and arises in response to the subject matter of man's thinking. "Here lies," Ott writes in *Denken und Sein,* "the key to understanding the whole of Heidegger's work and the key to the whole relevance of this thinker for theology." [59]

Ott, using the key supplied by Heidegger, points out that it is language which articulates, and is inseparable from, the picture of reality impressed upon us as we participate in

history. It is *through* our language that the myth of history
is transmitted to us by our culture. Just as we have tried to
understand that we do not stand outside history as something which we have at our disposal, so too in authentic
thinking we do not stand outside of the language which
enables that thinking to take place. Language, like history,
is that which is granted to us, and enables us to understand
ourselves. All men take their stand in language, and speak
from there; and those who participate in the myth of history
take their stand in the language of history, and speak from
there. "Even the simplest historical argument is after all
basically a linguistic occurrence, an encounter with spoken
or written utterances," [60] and only this linguistic encounter
or dialogue constitutes authentic historical knowledge.[61]
Following from this, Ott can speak of the witnesses brought
together in the canon of Holy Scripture as "the 'linguistic
room,' the universe of discourse, the linguistic net of co-
ordinates, in which the church has always resided and
moved in its faith, its preaching, its prayer, and also its
theology." [62] If, in opposition to this, there is the misunderstanding of history in terms of objectively given facts which
are at our disposal, this is a parallel to the rationalistic misunderstanding of language as a "tagging" of objective
things, or as a "shorthand" for ideas at which we have
arrived independently of language. This is the "thought
which does not think." If, on the other hand, the understanding of history and language which has been developed
by Vico, Heidegger, Ott, and others is accepted, then the
place of "objective facts" is seen to be the same as that of
linguistic "tags": they are both secondary abstractions developed from and dependent upon the primordial, mythic
phenomenon of language and history. It is as a consequence
of such considerations as these that Ott maintains: "We
are coming to discover with increasing clarity that the
problem of the historicity of existence, the problem of
hermeneutics, and the problem of language are in the last

analysis one and the same." [63] It should be emphasized
here, however, that for Ott the relationship of history and
language is a problem. For Ott "the big question has become: What really happens when a *word* or a *thought* oc-
curs?" [64] We have learned that they are not information
but event. Now, therefore, it is our "theological task to
clarify the event-character of the word in terms of the Biblical word and the event-character of the theological thinking
involved in it in terms of the great thoughts of the theological tradition. I do not doubt that in this matter we are still
at the beginning." [65]

WORD OF GOD AND WORD OF MAN

The "beginning" of which Ott speaks has been well advanced by Gerhard Ebeling, and especially in regard to the
significance of the phrases "Word of God" and "Word of
man" for language, history, and theology. Before entering
into a discussion of this, however, it will be useful to point
out some of the essential points at which Ebeling's theology
is congruent with that of Ott.

First, Ebeling is thoroughly and consistently aware that
the function of language in conveying information is a secondary and derivative one, and that the primary function of
language is the performatory one in which it articulates the
speaker's humanity in both its individual and its corporate
aspects. "So we do not get at the nature of words by asking
what they contain, but by asking what they effect, what they
set going, what future they disclose [for man]." [66] Second,
it follows from this that *"The primary phenomenon in the
realm of understanding is not understanding OF language
[X means Y, etc.], but understanding THROUGH language.
. . . the word is what opens up and mediates understanding, i.e., brings something to understanding."* [67] Understanding language means, first of all, to render it "luminous."
Third, Ebeling like Ott repeatedly affirms the linguisticality

of existence. Thus, "man is the being who has language," [68]
and "existence is existence through word and in word." [69]
Fourth, since Ebeling understands existence as being historical in nature, the affirmation of the linguisticality of
existence carries with it the affirmation of the profoundly
interrelated nature of language and history, and points toward what we have called an "erotics of history." "I do not
merely in a factual sense *have* a past and a future like all
temporal things, but I also *know* of this. It is solely through
language that I can have a relation to past and future, that
past and future are present to me, that I can go back behind
my present and stretch out ahead of it." [70]

However, Ebeling's position is not merely a different
statement of that held by Ott, but also serves to advance
the task of contemporary theology by its more detailed
attention to what is meant by "word of God" and "word of
man."

The driving passion behind the work of Gerhard Ebeling
is the yearning to be able to speak responsibly about God.
It is Ebeling's contention that the word "God" has "sub-
sided into speechlessness, or has been suppressed in super-
ficial talk." [71] In the face of this situation we are called
upon to play our part in letting the word of God "rescue
God himself from anonymity and pseudonymity" by bringing God to linguistic expression.[72] This concern is not a
concern for the vocable "God." Rather, says Ebeling with
the passion and refreshing directness which underlies and
repeatedly breaks through in his work, the word "God" is
used not for its own sake, "but in order to save man from
choking on his own self because he no longer has any word
with which to cry out of the depths of his self-contradiction
and call upon the mystery that surrounds him." [73] The
"enormity" of our present responsibility toward the world
in this matter is driven home as we find ourselves caught
in the tension between, on the one hand, the tradition, the
Catholic substance, for which we are responsible; and, on
the other hand, the necessity of holding ourselves open to

the "tempestuous vehemence of our age, which is the place of present responsibility." [74]

It is in response to this situation that Ebeling wishes to resensitize us to, and make us cognizant of, the power of the word of God which now operates in anonymity and pseudonymity, and which is diminished thereby.[75] Insofar as we are caught up in this power, we are caught up in the power, the reality, of God himself—God is "rescued," that is, we are rescued. The "central point in our deliberations on hermeneutics," writes Ebeling, is "that 'word' itself has a hermeneutic character and hermeneutics is the theory of 'word.'" [76] Word itself has an interpretive character, or carries interpretation within it. Language "speaks." Man does not "have" language, it is not something which is at his disposal; rather, "man takes his stand in speech and talks from there." [77]

This, of course, places a very high valuation upon word and language. It is for this reason that we have discussed at length the understanding of language which is operative in Ott and Ebeling (and before them in Buber, Vico, and Heidegger). Since word, and pre-eminently word of God, has this critical position, just what is this word of God? In answer to this question, we would insist with Ebeling that "word" in the two expressions, "God's word" and "man's word," refers to the same thing. It is a fundamental misunderstanding when we conceive of God's word as being "so to speak a separate class of word alongside the word spoken between men, which is otherwise the only thing we usually call word." [78] Rather: "When the Bible speaks of God's Word, then it means here unreservedly word as word —word that as far as its word-character is concerned is completely normal, let us not hesitate to say: natural, oral word taking place between man and man." [79] And elsewhere he states that "from the standpoint of the manner of its encounter, God's word as word is identical with the natural, human, spoken word." [80]

In order to avoid unnecessary confusion, let it be said

here immediately that Ebeling, in line with traditional theology, *also* wishes to distinguish between the word of God and the word of man. This distinction, however, is made not upon the basis of word as word, but upon the basis of who is the real speaker of it: "God, who alone is *verax,* or man, who is *mendax* (Rom. 3:4)." [81] In the former case the word speaks of and gives truth and life; in the latter case it speaks of and gives untruth and death. As far as word as word is concerned, however, God's word and man's word are the same. Word is what unites God and man; it is what God and man have in common.

This aspect of Ebeling's understanding of word is crucial for his position in regard to the relationship of faith and language, and in order to help clarify its importance he sets forth a widely held alternative. This alternative sets out from the presupposition that language is wholly a creation of man, and pertains only to him. Consequently, "word of man" is the norm for all that word is or can be. It follows, unavoidably, that the "word of God" can be understood only as somehow opposed to the "word of man"; and, further, if we are to have "word of God" at all, then it can be understood only as being in the "shadowy, unreal and veiled form of a human word." [82] This being the case, when we come to those human words which are said to be the word of God, we must then go on and say either that these words came into existence under supra-mundane conditions, and therefore must be interpreted in a corresponding way; or, that "God's Word and human words are related as kernel and husk, as eternally valid content and temporally conditioned form." [83] In either case, the rendering luminous of the word which unites God and man becomes impossible. Not only are these illusory and misleading solutions, but, before that, the problem of how God's word can be transformed into human words is an illusory problem. For, with all of its seeming reasonableness, this approach labors under the strange delusion that God speaks some language unknown and incomprehensible to us, which then must be translated into human language.[84] "X really *means* A."

This orientation to the problem would be appropriate if from man's perspective the fundamental characteristic of God had to do with his hiddenness and separation from us. This Ebeling denies, and, we hope, the whole understanding of history and language which we have built up in the preceding chapters lends support to his denial. The basis of Ebeling's denial is explicitly christological:

But if we take seriously the fact that God turns to man, claims him, addresses him, then it is meaningless to ask how he can do this in a way that man can understand. For this turning to man is God's humanity. His Word which is directed to man is as such a human word. There is no trace of a difference.[85]

Therefore,

"Word of God" is not just a symbolic mode of speech, which could perhaps be better replaced by the vaguer concept of "revelation." But the concept, the "Word of God," properly understood, provides the most striking expression of what happens to man from the side of God, that is to say, for the way in which God deals with man. For with God word and deed are one: his speaking is the way of his acting.[86]

Because God's speaking is his way of acting, and because of the linguistic-historical nature of reality, the hermeneutical process of understanding cannot be completed apart from the event of proclamation. Very concisely, Ebeling states it this way: "The problem of theological hermeneutics would not be grasped without the inclusion of the task of proclamation; it is not until then that it is brought decisively to a head at all." [87] "The task of proclamation." How much is summed up in this phrase! It follows naturally from Ebeling's passion for the restitution of the word of God that his thought culminates in an affirmation of the necessity of the effective proclamation of the word of God. Language is the House of Being which comes into being in the meeting, the language-event, which takes place between God and man. Language not only describes, but, more significantly, bodies forth that encounter. Or, drawing upon Robinson's very penetrating way of putting it, we may say that language does not simply describe the event as it happened (in which case it would again be a case of *bruta facta*), but also the event happened as it was described because the description is what is *meant*. Here "meaning" has lost the form-destroying quality to which, as we have seen, Sontag so emphatically objects.[88] The language-event results in, or better "is," an ecstatic confirmation of meaning for those who participate in it; a "meaning" which is not "behind" the form of the words, but which emerges in the "really accurate, sharp, loving description" constituted by the words (given and received) which body forth the event. Word comes out of relationship and lives in relationship; it is found *between* man and man, *between* God and man. In Buber's terms, word is essentially a *Thou*-saying. "Word," says Ebeling,

is therefore rightly understood only when it is viewed as an event which—like love—involves at least two. The basic structure of word is therefore not statement—that is an abstract variety of the word-event—but apprisal, certainly not in the colourless sense of information, but in the pregnant sense of participation and communication.[89]

And, *the* word event, the original relational event which brings reality into being, is the encounter with Jesus of Nazareth.

In time the language which has bodied forth the encounter between man and man, between man and God, becomes Scripture, becomes a "text." The text still carries a potency, the potency of the relational event which brought it into being; but the potency of meeting and meaning has slipped back into the I-It of report and information, for "the real, filled present, exists only in so far as actual presentness, meeting and relation exist." [90] Nevertheless, the reality of the relational event reported in the text is not somehow "behind" the text, but *in* the text; and can only be approached *through* the text as it becomes luminous in the event of proclamation, whether in sermon, in liturgy, or in some less formal mode of encounter and relationship.[91] In any case, the description of the event is what is meant; and just as the original appropriation of the event did not take place apart from the language which describes it, so our re-appropriation of *that* event will not take place apart from *that* language—however "mythical." If word is what unites God and man, it is also that which in the event of proclamation unites past and present, and which assures us that we will be able to take past and present with us into the future. It is especially this future-oriented aspect of word which makes us aware that word includes the dimension of promise: in the present, word promises our continued relationship to the confirmation of meaning in our past, thus enabling us to be attentive toward it; and word also promises our continuing relationship to this confirmation of meaning in a series of successive fulfillments of meaning as we go into the future.[92] From beginning to end, existence is existence through word and in word.[93]

Ebeling's statements about the event of proclamation are supported and extended by Ernst Fuchs's own distinctive and provocative discussion of the same area. Fuchs speaks of proclamation in terms of his concept of the "hermeneutical principle." This concept includes a recognition of the role of "pre-understanding" (i.e., the orientation to experience which the individual brings to the text or event). However, Fuchs seeks to describe historical understanding in greater depth than is possible when the *individual's pre-understanding,* with its inevitable tendency to stress the rational and the "inviolable ego," is emphasized. As a corrective to the concept of pre-understanding, Fuchs's "hermeneutical principle" states that if the historical text or event is to be understood, then it must be brought into a situation in which it is able to "speak." This situation is referred to as the "place." Fuchs uses the limited but useful analogy of placing a cat before a mouse; in such a situation the cat "speaks," i.e., "catness" is manifested (comes into being at a certain time and in a certain fashion) and understood.[94] This is the "place" of truth. Analogously, the "place" of truth for the historical text comes into being when it is placed before man in such a way that through the act of speaking he responds to the text in the light of his own concrete, care-full and anxious situation. When this takes place truth, or better, language, breaks through; not in the sense, of course, of a rote repetition of the form of the text, but in the sense that the situation described by the text is affirmed by the speaker to be his own concrete situation, and as calling for his decision in response to it. The hermeneutical principle directs us to this "place" which "bestows on understanding the power and truth of an *occurrence*. It is the *power* of understanding in the birth of *the language naming the truth*." [95] Once again it is brought home to us that the historical process is basically a linguistic process.[96]

We may say, therefore, that the aim of proclamation is to enable that language to take place which again and again names the truth of the text as being the truth of the speaker's own present, concrete situation. Thus, in the interpretation or understanding of the text it is not first of all the past, but *"it is really the present that is interpreted with the help of the text."* [97] And here, as always, "present" is understood as the "eschatologically given present."

So it is that man's linguistically formed self-understanding (pre-understanding) stands at the beginning of the process of historical proclamation; but even more significant is the linguistically formed self-understanding which emerges at the end of the proclamation and interpretation. This is true of historical interpretation generally, but most decisively it is true of the interpretation of the word of God, at the end of which "the man who is addressed understands himself anew, in that he receives himself from God as a new creature." [98] This Fuchs can aptly refer to as a " 'sacramental' happening." [99]

What, then, are the distinguishing marks of proclamation; or, how do we know when proclamation has taken place? The proclamation of the word of God presupposes the word of man; the ability of man to recognize within the familiar context of his existence that something is being spoken *to him,* and thus to enter into relationship through the spoken word.[100] But *into* this familiar context the word of God comes as "the announcement of what is hidden," [101] and is received in such a way that this announcing of what is hidden "is understood as altering the [familiar] context through the presence of what is hidden." [102] This alteration does not violate the context of man's life, but by bringing to light what is needful in the situation the word of God rectifies and verifies that context. This is why "the more fruitful form for disclosing the word's power to awaken understanding is not to spew forth platitudes but rather to allude to something that provokes reflection" [103] and participation. The parables of Jesus are a perfect example of this process; and Ebeling's and Fuchs's respective analyses are provocative reflection upon what is taking place in Jesus' parables.

Surprise (or grace), the announcement of what is needful, the rectification of man's situation—these are the distinguishing marks of the proclamation of the word of God, the "one single thing" which results in making "man human by making him a believer, i.e., a man who confesses to God as his future and therefore does not fail his fellowmen in the one absolutely necessary and salutary thing, *viz.* true word." [104] What a powerful expression of the communion of saints this is! This "good, beneficent, saving, illuminating

Word" men owe to one another, albeit that we so often do not say it and find that it is not proclaimed to us. But where it is proclaimed, the word is received as a promise of God, for

A promise means a pledge from one to another regarding the future. The Word as an event is always something said from one to another, as it were he carries his saying to the other, so that it is with him, or he is with the matter which is being spoken about. The Word which is concerned with God would then in this sense say God to us, so that God comes to the one addressed and is with him, and the one addressed is with God. All talk of God in which this does not happen would not be real talk of God.[105]

CONCLUSIONS

To what extent does the understanding of language, history, and myth presented in this chapter represent an advance upon Bultmann's treatment of these same areas? Does the new hermeneutic lay the foundation for an erotics of language and history?

There are many obvious points of similarity between the new hermeneutic and Bultmann: the concern with language which will communicate, the emphasis upon proclamation and decision, the necessity of discovering the *present* significance of texts and traditions, the general drawing upon existential categories, and much else.

The differences between the new hermeneutic and Bultmann, however, are equally significant. The most significant and far-reaching of these differences is a new sensitivity to language, and to the relationship between language and history. It is this which finds expression in the term "language-event" (or "word-event"). It is the intention of this term to clarify language by pointing to its *event*-character, and hence to its participation in, and its being informed by, what we have called the myth of history. Language which participates in the myth of history has the performatory power to

grant the reality or "true story" around which the community of history forms. Simultaneously, the term "language-event" intends to clarify history by pointing out how
it is informed by the tradition and experience of language
of those who participate in the myth of history.

When language and history are approached in this way,
then the interpretation *of* language ("X really *means* A.")
is replaced by the interpretation *through* language, i.e., the
really accurate, sharp, loving description of an event in
all its luminosity. Here the possibility of an erotics of language and history is opened up; a fundamental reversal in
which we renounce the infirm glory of the positivist describing of things as they "actually happened," and begin to understand that at least to some extent the event happened as
it is described, because the description is what is meant.
This *is,* admittedly, an interpretation of language and history; a new hermeneutic, if you wish; but it is an interpretation or hermeneutic which shows *how* an event is what it is,
rather than showing what it *means.* In Vico's language, this
approach recognizes that the "nature of an event" (what it
means) can be understood in no better way than through
a description of how it "came into being at a certain time
and in a certain fashion." There is present in this approach
to language and event the new possibility of really being
attentive to and rendering luminous what man has created
(the *factum*) in the past, in all of its concrete "whatness."

It is from this position that we would agree with Fuchs
that "the controversy about demythologization was not
thought out to a conclusion, because the premise on both
sides remained too similar. I mean the concept of the *fact of
salvation* (*Heilstatsache*), which is found in Bultmann." [106]
That is, complains Fuchs, if we follow Bultmann's procedure, we only replace one rationalistic objectification or
abstraction with another; for example, the mythological
"fact" of the Resurrection is replaced by the manifestation
of the possibility of "authentic existence." This procedure,
while it does away with "fact" in the usual positivist sense,

still leaves us with "fact" of salvation perceived by faith, in
a process of abstraction, to lie *behind* the mythological
statements found in the historical record. In either approach, the false disjunction between *Historie* and *Geschichte,* which has had such a devastating effect upon
Christian faith, remains intact. Abstracting thought, the
"thought which does not think," still reigns supreme over
word and event.

In contrast, the approach to language and history which
we have explored in this chapter neither objectifies (ab-
stracts) in the positivist manner of establishing "facts," nor
in the manner of those who would seek the significance
which supposedly resides behind the "facts" of history. Instead, renouncing the false disjunction between *Historie* and
Geschichte, the strictest attention is paid to the event of
language, through which there is the ecstatic confirmation
of meaning, the granting of being.

We are aware that an erotics of language and history may
be threatening to many because it lacks the "control" which
traditionally has been supplied by the "facts" that are at the
historian's disposal. This is true; such control is lacking,
and indeed, as we have argued, never existed except within
the narrowly and arbitrarily delimited realm of secondary
abstractions formed by "objective facts." However, it is
worth stating again what we have argued previously: an
erotics of language and history is not a Hard Perspectivism
in which all historical assertions are of equal value; nor is
the *distinction* and tension between *Historie* and *Geschichte*
obliterated; nor is the methodological discipline of history
any less rigorous. Quite to the contrary, it is only as we
recognize ourselves as standing within the myth of history,
and including the recognition of the intimate part language
plays in taking this stand, that we gain the freedom to act
and think within the true bounds, i.e., within the bounds set
by the "true story" of history.

Insofar as mythology has come to express a false objectificátion and rationalization of experience, then, we have agreed, it must be broken or demythologized. Similarly, the misunderstanding of history in terms of clear and distinct ideas or facts calls for the breaking or demythologization of this false objectification and rationalization of experience. In both of these situations, man falsely understands himself in terms of objectification and abstraction. Or, he creates a mythology about himself in which he objectifies and rationalizes, and thereby attempts to control, his own existence and the existence of others. He sees himself separated from the language and history which constitute his own existence. This idolatrous mythology needs to be demythologized in order that man may understand that history, which *in its very idea* is of God, addresses man, enabling him to "understand himself anew, in that he receives himself from God as a new creature." [107] Thus, Fuchs remarks with both profundity and wit: "Who is now the object of demythologization? Neither God, nor Jesus, nor the world . . . but rather man caught up in a distorted relation to himself." [108]

5

The Fullness of Real Mutual Action

Orthodox Christian faith has always been concerned to apprehend, to address, and to protect the personal reality which, although it is not at our disposal, moves into personal encounter with us on the road to Damascus, on the Hill Difficulty, in Tegel prison, in the Eucharist, wherever— the personal reality which is named "God," "Father," "Son," "Holy Spirit." As in all personal encounter, this encounter is marked by mutuality and action: the mutuality of address and response; the action of address and response. Even in its most objectivized and mythological forms, traditional formulations of the Christian faith have sought to affirm this personal reality; and this intention is correct, however deficient the execution may have been from time to time. From the beginning of our inquiry it has been affirmed that the encounter with God as *personal* reality is part of biblical and, implicitly, of historical experience. We now wish to turn to a more thorough discussion of this affirmation.

Gordon Kaufman, in a recent and provocative essay, "On the Meaning of 'God': Transcendence without Mythology," [1] deals in a fresh and helpful way with a question closely related to our own: How may we speak about God in terms of personal encounter, but without entering into a mythological or metaphysical dualism? Kaufman writes: "We must find a way in the present situation to restate (in terms not simply presupposing the old dualistic mythology) the contention that the ultimate reality [God] with which

124

man has to do is somehow 'beyond' that which is directly given in experience." [2] Kaufman then attacks this problem by investigating the function of "God-language," and finds that this language "arises because certain features of our experience force us up against the limit(s) of all possible knowledge and experience," [3] and without this experience God-language would not arise. "In this respect the idea of God functions as a *limiting concept,* i.e., a concept which does not primarily have content in its own right drawn directly out of a specific experience but which refers to that which we do *not* know but which is the ultimate limit of all our experiences." [4] Here it is important to emphasize that "limit means *limit,*" and that most modern men no longer believe it is justified to proceed from our experience of limit to a spelling out in some detail of the reality which is said to lie beyond this limit, say, in terms of mythological stories.[5] "We begin then with a somewhat different duality than that of two-world thinking: the duality of experience and its Limit(s)." [6]

Kaufman identifies what he believes to be four fundamental types of limiting experience: (1) the external physical limitation of physical objects; (2) the organic limitations of our own powers; (3) "the external *personal* limitation of other selves engaged in activities and programs running counter to our own" (which limitation, because it involves volition and intention, is "neither simply internal nor external but is interpersonal and social" [7]); and (4) the experience of *normative* constraints expressed in such distinctions as true-false, real-illusory, good-bad etc., which "appear to the self not to be its own spontaneous creations but to impinge upon it with categorical demands and claims." [8] Kaufman argues convincingly that the "imagery built into the notion of limit by its physical origins reminds us that every *actual* limit or boundary which marks off and restricts *real being* (in contrast to, for example, a mathematical limit or similar abstract "limiting idea") must itself be conceived *as a reality, as having some kind of sub-*

stance and structure." [9] The experience of limit is the
awareness of that which limits *me,* my being; and "thus in
some sense an actual 'encounter' with that which *limits
me.*" [10] It is also part of this experience that we can never
get beyond this limit, and therefore we can only imaginatively construct its substance and structure out of elements
known more fully in our experience—as, for example, a
man in a prison cell which he had never left and could
never leave, would imaginatively construct the substance
and structure of the walls which constrict him by analogy
with the experienceable objects within his cell.[11]

How do we proceed from such particular experiences of
being limited to the notion of being "bounded on all sides,"
the experience of "finitude," the ultimate Limit? Not, says
Kaufman, through the immediate experience of ultimate
Limit (i.e., not through some fifth type of limiter), but
through a process of reflecting and generalizing upon our
diverse particular experiences of being limited. This process
is the experiential ground "both of theological conceptions
[including the concept of history] and of the nontheistic
metaphysical schemas as well." [12] Only in this way could
the concept of finitude develop. Such concepts, however,
are not empty ideas; they grasp the Limit "as concrete
actuality impinging on us, i.e., not merely abstractly but as
having some concrete character or nature"; [13] as "that which
in fact constricts and constrains the actual concrete self." [14]

What *is* this Limit, then, which "constricts and constrains" us? The answer to this question, if we are not going
to resort to the mythological claim to possess direct knowledge of a fifth type of limit not within our experience, will
have to be conceived of in terms of one or more of the
four types of limits which we have mentioned: physical,
organic, personal, and normative. Each of the four types of
finite limit has certain claims to make as being *the* source
of images for conceiving of the Limit, and none can be
conclusively shown to be *the* model. Consequently, one's
model will be more or less arbitrarily chosen—or at least

so it appears to one observing rather than participating in such a decision.[15]

Upon the basis of this careful preparation, Kaufman asserts:

When a personal limiter is the analogical basis for understanding the ultimate Limit, a doctrine of God results. The ultimate Limit is then conceived in quasi-personal terms to be understood most decisively with notions drawn originally from the language used to deal with interpersonal experience. It is clear that this conception is the one operative in the biblical tradition where God is spoken of as lord, father, judge, king, etc., and he is said to love, hate . . . to be characterized by mercy, forgiveness . . .—all terms drawn from the linguistic region of interpersonal discourse.[16]

To this assertion we would wish to add our own: "When a personal limiter is the analogical basis for understanding the ultimate Limit, a doctrine of history—the understanding of reality as historical—results." However, our statement, like Kaufman's, needs to be qualified; for it is only when the analogy of the personal limiter is taken with radical seriousness, that a biblical doctrine of God and of history results. Thus, in the account of the avatars of Krishna, or in the Bodhisattva theology of Mahayana Buddhism, the analogy of the personal limiter is present, but it is understood as being only *provisionally* valid: a stage on the way to the *restitutio in integrum*. It is only in biblical religion, and above all within the community of the Incarnation, that this analogy is taken with complete seriousness. The experience of the Limit in terms of the analogy of the personal limiter is what is being articulated in the Bible and in the historical understanding of reality. Thus, as we have seen, Kaufman characterizes the perception of experience in terms of the personal limiter as being one in which experience is seen in terms of "the clash of wills, decisions, and purposes" (as manifested, for example, in the tension between promise and fulfillment), and "precisely because [these] matters of volition and intention are subjective, this experience is neither simply internal nor external but is interpersonal and social." [17] Moreover, we would add, because this experience is "interpersonal" and "social," it is therefore intrinsically "linguistic." In these statements we have either explicitly or implicitly, and in language only slightly different from our own, the major structural elements of the historical understanding of reality which we have described in the preceding chapters. Kaufman's statements are, indeed, a brief but excellent description of the dynamics of historical experience! Consequently, we would say that the historical understanding of reality also understands the Limit in terms of the analogy of the personal limiter.

Our extension of Kaufman's thesis is supported by the similarities between the way in which he develops his position and the way in which we have described historical experience. Thus, Kaufman's claim (*not* a "truth" claim) that the use of the personal limiter in theism gives it a certain "flexibility and breadth" which enables it "to deal with the considerable diversity of types of finite limiter somewhat more easily, perhaps" than when other limiters are taken as the model, is a claim which is often made for history also.[18] Like theism, the historical understanding of reality is guided by the personal limiter, and consequently has the flexibility and inclusiveness characteristic of personal relationships, a quality which is not possessed by perceptions of reality guided by the physical, organic, or normative limiters. The reverse side of the flexibility and inclusiveness of history, is that its perception of experience lacks those "clear and distinct ideas" which are possible when, for example, the world is perceived in terms of the limiting norms which find expression in mathematics.

Even more significantly, the similarity holds in regard to the critical issue of language. In his own, more sober, way Kaufman describes what is very like the new hermeneutic's "word-event" or "language-event." He points out that in the encounter with other persons we encounter a reality, "the active center of the self." This reality lies beyond the physiologically based perception of the other person, and is communicated to us "in and through the language which we jointly speak." [19]

It is in the act of communication that we discover that the other is more than merely physical being, is a conscious self; it is in the experience of speaking and hearing that we come to know the *personal* hidden behind and in the merely physical. This is the most powerful experience we have of *transcendence of the given* on the finite level, the awareness of genuine activity and reality *beyond* and *behind* what is directly open to our view.[20]

This communication of the self, Kaufman emphasizes, just as we have from time to time, is not at our disposal; it must "come to us," and its self-communication does not result in the clear and distinct perception which would give us control over the self. It is this finite, linguistic experience of human self-communication (the personal limiter) which provides, in a way the other limiters cannot, the model for building the "image of inaccessible transcendence and freedom made known and effective through explicit acts of communication and power—through words and deeds—" which we use in our discourse with and about God.[21] The perception of the self in human encounter enables us to perceive the divine Self; or, in Buber's terms, the encounter with the Thou enables us to perceive the Eternal Thou.

This very rich presentation, with which we are clearly very much in sympathy, calls for a number of critical observations, although we wish to make it clear at the outset that these criticisms do not invalidate what we take to be the substance of Kaufman's proposal.

First, Kaufman maintains that "Organic, physical, and normative limiters can all be interpreted exhaustively in terms of what is given in and to experience (though it is not essential to do so), and it is mythology, therefore, if

one speaks of a transcendent extra-experiential reality on
the basis of one of those models; a personal limiter alone
necessarily and intrinsically involves genuine transcendence." [22] It would be helpful to see Kaufman elaborate
this with specific examples, for it is not clear that *this contrast* between personal limiters and other limiters will hold.
Presumably Kaufman means, for example, that the physical
or organic limiter of birth, growth, decay, and rebirth
operative in Mesopotamian and other religions may be
interpreted exhaustively in terms of what is given to experience, and therefore *any* talk of the transcendent extra-
experiential reality which comes to expression in these
physical limiters is mythology. It is not apparent that this is
so; certainly those who have participated in such religions
in the past and in the present would not say so. A positivistic approach to experience can "explain" *both* the cycles
of nature *and* human encounter strictly in terms of what is
given to finite experience, but neither is convincing unless
the presuppositions of the "explanations" are accepted be-
forehand. Admittedly (or is this just our Western, theistic
bias at work?), physical limiters are more susceptible to a
positivistic analysis; nevertheless, the significance for man
of the natural or physical world is not evident in terms of
finite experience. It is interesting in this connection that the
divine beings who characteristically participate in the
annual cycle of nature constitute, in effect, an introduction
of the personal limiter as a *secondary* model.

Second, and closely related to what we have just said,
what is the *formal* difference between the theistic positing of
a "genuine activity and reality *beyond* and *behind* what is
directly open to our view" in personal encounter,[23] and the
positing by Mesopotamian religion for example, of the
genuine reality *beyond* and *behind* what is directly open to
our view of the annual cycle of nature? Admittedly, the
choice of model and image makes a profound difference as
to what is understood; but that the theistic approach is intrinsically "nonmythological," and that other approaches

are intrinsically "mythological," is not clear. Both start from images drawn from the finite world, and neither, even in their most extreme "otherworldly" formulations, completely lose sight of the this-worldly reference of their imagery. Regardless of the type of imagery or limiters used, that which is objectionable about "mythology" is the dualism which results when, *losing sight of the fact that the closest we can come to reality is in our images or myths,* we assert that our imagery or myth is a description of an objective reality which exists in some "other world." As is well known, this dualism brings with it such liabilities as the false sense of security about one's images, since they, so it is thought, are only descriptions of what exists objectively; a temptation to believe that since we can objectively describe ultimate reality, therefore we are in a position to control it (magic); and an insensitivity and spirit of arrogance in our confrontation with other religions which are not "true" or objective, as ours is, but only "mythological"! It is evident, as Kaufman points out, that this dualism or mythology springs up in all religions, including theistic ones. We would also most certainly agree with Kaufman's perceptive argument that the personal limiter operative in theistic imagery is less prone to a dualistic mythology. What is not clear, however, is that all imagery which is not dominated by the personal limiter is *intrinsically* and necessarily mythological in the negative sense which we have just discussed. It is not evident that the participants in Mesopotamian religion, for example, consistently saw their religious statements in an objectifying, dualistic way. We would prefer to say, drawing upon the distinction which we stated earlier, that both theistic religions with their personal limiter, and nontheistic religions which use physical, organic, and other limiters, are equally *mythic* perceptions of the world; and that, further, all mythic perceptions of the world are liable to development in a *mythological* direction. The continued recognition of the mythic element in theism in general, and Christianity in particular, enables us to

recognize a limited but important unity between ourselves
and other religions, including those of the ancient past. The
retention of "myth" and "mythic" should also be a reminder
to us that mythology is not totally wrong, but only a per-
version of an important perception of mythic speaking and
thinking; namely, that in the development of our imagery we
find ourselves compelled in one way or the other to posit
something objectively "beyond" the imagery. Kaufman himself speaks, as we have seen, of "genuine activity and reality
beyond and *behind* what is directly open to our view." [24]
Let us give mythology its due: Mythology, including portions of Scripture and liturgy which have been developed in
a mythological direction, perceives very clearly the necessity
of the "beyond and behind." What mythology does not
perceive, as Kaufman says in effect, is that the closest we
can approach reality, the "beyond and behind," is in our
images. This is the point which is constantly stressed by the
new hermeneutic and, earlier, by Vico. *Verum et factum
convertuntur:* "the true and the made are convertible,"
and above all else, it is language which is *made* by man.

THE ORIGINAL RELATIONAL EVENT

Up to this point our discussion of Kaufman's essay has
concentrated on what he has said concerning "limiters"
and "the Limit." This subject is, however, complemented
by a second: the constitutive, historically mediated *image*
which gives any particular Limit its transcendent reference.[25] Although a complete description of what is involved
in this matter of the historically mediated image is beyond
the bounds that Kaufman has set for his essay, he does
sketch it in because it completes his analysis of "limitation."
We would like to conclude our discussion of Kaufman's
essay by describing briefly what he sees as being involved
in the historically mediated image, and then commenting
upon it. The transition from "limitation," language, history, etc. in the first part of Kaufman's essay, to the histori-

cally mediated image in the latter part, is just the transition which we wish to make in this chapter of our own investigation.

Kaufman ties these two matters together in the following way: "The constitutive *experience* underlying the word 'God' is that of limitation; the constitutive *image* which gives the term its peculiar transcendent reference is personalistic. These fused into one in the concretely religious apprehension of our finitude provide us with the root referent for the word." [26] Since the two are "fused into one," it is perhaps impossible to say that one or the other comes first. The problem for Jews and Christians, however, is *in what circumstances* does the fusion of the *experience* and the *image* which go to form our understanding of God, take place. Kaufman says that only when limitation is "grasped and interpreted in concrete personalistic terms does the Limit become understood as the expression of a being transcending our world, i.e., of an active God." [27] This grasping and interpreting of experience in personalistic terms is, of course, a "faith-interpretation" of our experience of limitedness.[28] We presume, however, that all people have had and do have *some* experience of the personal limiter. This is reflected, as we observed before, in the appearance of the personal limiter in a *subsidiary* role in many myths where the Limit is understood primarily in terms of the physical or other limiters. Consequently, it would seem that the experience of any one of the four specific limiters does not, by itself, yield the constitutive image; nor does the general experience of limitation arising out of our experience with the various limiters provide such an image. The question remains, then, as to the circumstances under which we both perceive our limitedness and finitude, and also are enabled to affirm that the imagery growing out of the personal limiter is the *constitutive* imagery which enables us to apprehend our limitedness and finitude as due to an active will over against us—that is, theism.

We are not sure how Kaufman would answer this ques-

tion. For our part, however, we would answer it in the
following way; and, as the ensuing discussion will indicate,
we believe that this way is consistent with Kaufman's position. We have seen how Kaufman maintains that the experience of finitude, on the one hand, and the constitutive
image (supplied by faith interpretation), on the other hand,
are "fused into one." [29] "The faith interpretation, of course,
is shaped by the concrete historical tradition within which
one stands." [30] For Jews and Christians, obviously, the
concrete historical tradition which determines our choice
of the personal limiter, as *the* limiter which alone is adequate to be the model for images of the Limit, is the ongoing biblical tradition, a tradition which for Christians
reaches its fullest expression in the encounter with Jesus of
Nazareth. It is this original relational event which determines the Christian's choice of the personal limiter and the
linguistic images associated with it. Further, it is this
original relational event which enables us to recognize that
the personal limiter known to all men is *the* model for our
images of the Limit.*

We believe that this is what Kaufman is saying, although
more abstractly, when he writes:

Only on the ground that God had in fact revealed himself
could it be claimed he exists; only if there were and is some
sort of movement from beyond the Limit to us, making known
to us through the medium of the Limit the reality of that which
lies beyond, could we be in a position to speak of such reality
at all; only if God actually "spoke" to man could we know there
is a God. It is of course the Christian claim that God has acted

* It follows from this, without retracting anything which we have said
in previous chapters, that just as all people have *some* experience of the
personal limiter, so they have *some* experience of what goes to make up
what we call history. Equally, just as only in biblical religion is the
personal limiter *the* model for the Limit, so only in biblically oriented experience is the christologically based myth of history seen as *the* model
for our understanding of reality. It is only when this latter situation comes
to pass that we experience what we have learned to call "history."

to reveal himself and continues to do so. . . . genuine knowledge of God could not be affirmed on any other basis than such
revelation.[31]

Here is the fullness of real mutual action: God's action in
address, and man's action in response. Only on the ground
that God has *in fact* (this is the "true story") revealed himself, can we claim that he exists. Genuine knowledge of God
for us cannot be affirmed on any other basis than this real
mutual speaking. We have pointed to this action of mutual
affirmation in a variety of ways: as Thou-saying, as the
union of God and man in "language-event," as the manifestation of love, as participation in the myth of history.
Although there is no *one* correct way of describing this
situation, Fuchs brings together in a beautiful way the
various elements present here.

Language is giving. It assimilates and acquires through its taking
place. When someone says "yes" he bestows that admission in
which he himself is imparted. So God says his "yes" not to
strangers but to his own, and in this he imparts himself as the
one who belongs to us. This is not an addition or application
which God makes of himself or adds to himself. It is the event in
which God himself takes place as love and so imparts love.
Therefore, because in the case of both God and man the "yes"
really permits understanding, I maintain that the "yes" is the
word of all words and that the Johannine ἐγώ εἰμί is that particular language-event in which God quite simply expressed himself as the word, as the "yes." Faith can wish only to correspond
to this, by holding fast on its part to what it has heard, and
making confession here and now to God's "yes" in the crucified
Christ.[32]

More recently Fuchs has commented upon this matter:

Yet what then does "word" mean? For we wish to achieve with
the term word the expression that is able to grasp Christ once

for all. In the supplement to my *Hermeneutik* I made the attempt to understand word as that Yes that forestalls and precedes every No, as the Yes ultimately constitutive of every language-event. For word is, after all, language; it speaks, as its very nature. In genuine language do we not, even before any affirmation, say simply this Yes, when we speak? And even more: With our language do we not correspond from the very first to a Yes that grants us entry, entry into that being in which we are with ourselves and yet precisely not left alone? Even though language usually alienates itself from the word, its ground, and builds all sorts of words that are only signs, does it not still in its own-most ground live from that Yes that is the word of all words? To be sure language would then be originally the language of God, and its basic trait would then rightly be named love.[33]

From this perspective it follows quite naturally that Fuchs's interpretation of John 1:1 reaches its completion in the translation: "In the beginning was the Yes, and the Yes was love, and love was the Yes." [34]

The fullness of real mutual action reaches its apotheosis in this Yes. Here, of course, the personal limiter is fully operative, for there is nothing more personal than affirmative speech. Nevertheless, in the speaking of this Yes, we arrive at that point where the awareness of our limitation and finiteness expressed in the language or imagery modeled upon the personal limiter approaches the disappearing point, and in its place arises the awareness of our entrance into the world-gathering and world-confirming reality which is Jesus of Nazareth. Here man and God come together. In the fullness of this mutual action, in this mutual speaking of Yes, it is recognized that words—and most specifically *this* Yes—are what God and man have in common. Here, in Jesus of Nazareth, God and man come together. This is the original relational event of the Christian faith, and it is only as a consequence of the similarly directed Yes-speaking of succeeding generations that the Christian faith is enabled to continue.

It follows from this, if our argument in the preceding chapters is in the main correct, that this mutual speaking of Yes brings the myth of history into being for us, and that only in the continued speaking of this Yes does the myth of history continue. This is not to say, as we made clear in Chapter 1, that history springs into being *ex nihilo* with Jesus Christ. However, we do wish to say that as the personal limiter became central for the Israelites, so the understanding of the historical nature of reality became increasingly central for them. Moreover, we wish to maintain that, in Jesus Christ, the fullness of mutual personal action is decisively revealed, and as a consequence the constitutive elements which go to make up the myth of history are fulfilled and focused: promise and fulfillment, history as the realm of God's rule, the great significance of the human and created order, the exaltation of man and his responsibility for the creation. Collectively these elements or affirmations constitute the myth of history, the "true story" of our experience. These affirmations, however, are already to some degree abstractions from the myth of history which finds its immediate and most fundamental expression in the original relational event, Jesus Christ—in his Yes, and in our responding Yes. It is this language-event of Jesus Christ which permits the myth of history to move right to the center and become for us the controlling picture of all human experience. This is the christological foundation of the myth of history.

CONCLUSIONS

This understanding of history helps us to deal with three interrelated problems which have recurred again and again in the preceding chapters: the relationship between event and interpretation; the relationship of the historical Jesus and the kerygmatic Christ; and the relationship between past, present, and future. We have seen how these problems have many dimensions, but one or more of these three basic problems have been central at every stage of our discussion. As we have explored these problems we have maintained a more-or-less-constant dialogue between theology and history, and as a result of this we hope it is clear that these three problems are all aspects of the more general problem: How do we, who conceive of ourselves and our world historically, understand our relationship to God? [35] This question we take to be a different and better focus for the complex set of issues often focused around the term "secularization."

We believe, first of all, that the understanding of history which we have advanced, and which we have called a christologically based myth of history, is helpful because it enables us to take *seriously* such statements as that in the Gospel of John: "In the beginning was the Word, and the Word was with God, and the Word was God. He was in the beginning with God; all things were made through him, and without him was not anything made that was made" (John 1:1-3). Either the "all things" made through the creative Word refers to the whole fabric of man's experience, or it refers to nothing at all. The word of God defines and affirms reality for us, and not our conception of reality the word of God.[36] For us the reality which is defined and affirmed by the word of God is not "religious" reality or some other sequestered form of reality, but precisely the whole fabric of reality understood as history which proceeds from the creative Word of God.[37] It is Buber's concise yet powerful expression of this fundamental position in such terms as the "original relational incident," the "ecstatic confirmation of meaning," the "fulness of real mutual action," and so on, which has led us to draw upon his work at so many points. In assuming this position it is evident that "it is part of the phenomenon of understanding that the ground of the understanding, being a point beyond which no further questioning is possible, confronts us with a decision." [38] In our case, the decision concerns the word of God and history. In part, this decision is made by us self-consciously and explicitly; and, in part, it is a decision which is already and repeatedly made, corporately and largely unconsciously, by those who accept the historical nature of reality. Our decision here is not one in which we affirm a special, supernatural history based upon a special, supernatural word of God. We would prefer to express it, rather, that the word of God is for us the true, proper, finally valid word; and that history is the true, proper, finally valid myth which manifests the word of God. This point of view sees the word of God as the foundation and continually transforming power of that which man makes in history. Because that which is made has this ultimate source, we are enabled to say with Vico that "the true and the made are convertible"; and that man achieves truth by attending to what he has made in history, and above all the language which he has made in history. Just as the word of God is integral to what is made, so also it is clearly implicit here that the word or spirit of man is not alien to the creation. Man is in the image of God, and co-creator with him in the whole work of creation, but above all in the creation of language. From this position it is possible "to maintain responsibly to all comers . . . that God's Word is the ultimate ground of understanding because it is here in the last analysis that word is encountered as word and understanding as understanding." [39]

Turning to more specific considerations, although closely related to what we have just said, we believe that the erotics of history which we have presented here advances theology's task in our time by demonstrating the inadequacy of the various dichotomies so familiar in the past generation and still in our own: form and content, fact and interpretation, *Historie* and *Geschichte*, word and faith, historical Jesus and kerygmatic Christ, history and myth, and so on. These and other such dichotomies are really the single unloving disjunction, or dichotomy, in which it is assumed that there are, on the one hand, clear and distinct historical events, or even "facts," which are at our disposal; and, on the other hand, insights, interpretations, theologies, and so on, which have no organic relationship to the "facts" which they purport to interpret. We have tried to show that this dichotomy falsifies the whole dynamic of historical understanding. It is the historical understanding of reality with its christological foundation which is primary, while the innumerable facts which this myth of history enables us to perceive and to manipulate (often very creatively) are secondary. This does not mean, as we have stated clearly, that historical facts do not have their own integrity. They do have this integrity; they may not be manipulated at the whim of the individual. However, they have this integrity *within the myth of history*. This myth enables phenomena to be loved adequately, and hence to be known effectually as "historical facts"; it enables this perception to continue in the present and into the future; and it establishes the criteria or rules of evidence for deciding what constitutes a valid historical argument. We may for a time, for purposes of analysis, consider historical facts, in the spirit of I-It, as independent things. When we do this, and leaving aside the moot question as to whether it is even possible to do this completely, it is important to recognize that historical facts so conceived are secondary abstractions, ultimately dependent upon their organic association with the myth of history. In short, a perception of historical fact is a faith perception. Fact and faith belong together in loving union, as do the other pairs of terms which are often misunderstood as a dichotomy: form and content, word and faith, event and interpretation, historical Jesus and kerygmatic Christ, and so on.

In terms of our earlier discussion of Kaufman's ideas

concerning limiters and the Limit, to assent to any of these dichotomies is to be unable, or to refuse, to see the personal limiter and the Limit to which it points as the medium of our encounter with God. Thus, to assent to these dichotomies, and most clearly and centrally the dichotomy between word and faith, is an attitude of unfaith.[40] The devastating effect of unfaith in assenting to the faithless dichotomy is that it threatens *our very perception* of the event itself. Word and faith (event and interpretation, historical Jesus and kerygmatic Christ) arise together, or they do not arise at all. Although he used a different terminology, Vico recognized this. His whole protest was that the dichotomy present in the Cartesian epistemology simply did not allow for the possibility of history. In terms of our own discussion, the events of history cannot be perceived *as events of history* apart from the christologically based myth of history. That this is so is obscured from us, it is worth repeating, because of the almost universal conviction in our society that history is "no myth," but the "true story of how things really are"! Hence, while it is obviously true that being a Christian does not in itself make one a better historian *than anyone else who shares the historical assumptions of our society,* without the christological-based myth of history there would be no history at all *in the sense* in which it is understood in our society.

Upon the basis of these considerations, we want to give specific attention to the relationship of the historical Jesus and the kerygmatic Christ. The problem raised by this particular expression (historical Jesus/kerygmatic Christ) of the dichotomy between word and faith has repeatedly been raised in our discussions. We have said that the perception of historical event is also a faith perception. Further, we have said that this is most clearly and centrally true in those cases where the historical event in question is man's creation of language, the word-event; for it is in language that man "takes his stand" and tells of how it is with himself and his world. We cannot approach reality any more directly than through the linguistic images used in speaking. At the same time, we have said that certain human words are also the word of God. Here we do not mean that some esoteric meaning behind the words is the word of God, but that the human words are themselves the word of God for those who take their stand in them and speak from there. In the Fourth Gospel, Jesus speaks to Martha: " 'I am the resurrection and the life; he who believes in me, though he die, yet shall he live, and whoever lives and believes in me shall never die. Do you believe this?' She said to him, 'Yes, Lord, I believe that you are the Christ, the Son of God, he who is coming into the world' " (John 11:25-27, RSV). In these and similar words of Jesus, in his parables, and in his life, death and resurrection, we have Jesus' Yes; the "word of all words," as Fuchs so aptly characterizes it. This Yes is a human word, yet as Christians we say *this human word* is also the word of God. This is understood to be the expression of the ultimate truth of our situation.[41]

Why have we made this decision about certain human (human-divine) words, and most particularly why have we made this decision about Jesus' Yes? The "answer" to this question is that our encounter with Jesus of Nazareth compels us to do so; he is the original relational event who defines reality—our selves and our world—for us; and, specifically, he defines our selves and our world as being historical in nature. Since we have made the decision to take our stand in this Yes as the ultimate ground of understanding, we cannot explain this decision except by pointing to the word event which brought it about. Hence we agree with Ebeling: "The relation between word and faith is the only contact between God and existence"; and that this relation is "unique, unrepeatable and indivisible." [42] Just as word and faith are indivisible, so are historical event and its interpretation indivisible. The paradigm for this is the original relational event of Jesus Christ. Here above all the unity between word and faith, between event and interpretation, is "unique, unrepeatable and indivisible." From this it follows for the Christian faith and the historical understanding of reality: "To the inseparable togetherness of the two natures in Christ there corresponds the never-ending togetherness of word and faith." [43] Here it emerges once again, and in a most fundamental way, that the myth of history is christologically based.

This approach to the two natures of Christ does not have the "clarity" of the radical christological positions (in either their ancient or their subsequent forms), which take one-half of Christ's divine-human nature and emphasize it to the point of partially or completely obscuring the other half. This "clarity" can only be achieved by artificially establishing a dualism between the two natures, and then opting for one or the other of the resulting abstractions. Our approach does have the great advantage, however, of being consistent with the New Testament witness to the unity of the two natures, a unity which is most clearly testified to in the New Testament affirmation of the continuity between the historical Jesus of Nazareth and the risen Christ proclaimed in the kerygma. In addition, our position has the advantage, and this is only to restate the first advantage in different words, of being consistent with a historical understanding of reality, which is never marked by the "clarity" of the clear and distinct idea, and is always involved in the rich ambiguity—the "coolness"—of the language of personal self-communication. In this context we can see the pertinence of one of Vico's central axioms concerning historical thinking: "The nature of institutions [historical things] is nothing but their coming into being (*nascimento*) at certain times and in certain fashions." [44] Thus, who is Jesus Christ? He is the man who came into being at the time and in the fashion described in the language of the New Testament—language which consists (when all is said and done) of what Jesus said and what was

said in response to him, either directly or in the traditions
of the Church. This language of address and response contains all that we can know about the nature (the "time" and
"fashion") of Jesus.

So one illuminates the other. Jesus illuminates the apostles' talk
and their talk illuminates Jesus' task [by describing it]. *This is
why I have in my own way renewed the question of the historical
Jesus.* Jesus himself had been God's word to which all clung, for
Jesus did not want to be or to be understood as anything other
than God's word, which entered into his daily life and began
here its work. He was this word, for *he let himself be heard at
precisely that place where God himself had begun to speak.
Jesus was God's word, if at that time the time for this word had
come! And that is what faith in Jesus believes, by believing in
the historical Jesus.*[45]

It only remains to deal with the third of the recurring
problems which we identified at the beginning of this
section: the relationship between past, present, and future.
Because this has been dealt with by implication in our
treatment of the first two problems, we believe we may state
our position on this last problem rather briefly. Here, we
would add, our concern is not with the speculative or more
strictly philosophical aspects of the relationship of past,
present, and future but, rather, with the historical problem
of the proper emphasis upon, and relationship of, these
three dimensions of our experience.

We dealt with this problem most extensively within the
context of our examination of Bultmann's theology in
Chapter 3. We said there that Bultmann conceives of the
problem both correctly and helpfully in terms of the joining
of the "yield of the past" and the "promise of the future"
in the present, existential moment of decision. We saw,
however, that the way in which he works out this conception
is uneven. His statement of the "now" and "for me" aspects
of historical and faith assertions is correct and powerful, as

is his stress upon the future-oriented dimension of history and theology. His treatment of the "yield of the past," however, is inadequate, and consequently leads to an imbalance between past, present, and future in which the "whatness" of the past is largely reduced to a "thatness." This inadequate stress upon, and consequent lack of attentiveness toward, the "yield of the past," moreover, is intimately tied to an inadequate recognition of the community, which has produced the "yield of the past" and has transmitted this to the "now" of our own time. Further, we located the source of this inadequacy as residing in Bultmann's qualified yet continuing adherence to a Cartesian view of history of facts plus interpretation—*Historie* and *Geschichte*. We have argued at length, and need not repeat those arguments here, that in this misunderstanding of history in which the dichotomy between event and interpretation is initially predicated, it is subsequently impossible to reunite them. In this situation the existential "now," so essential as an element of history, tyrannizes over the whole of history as the individual treats of the past according to the exigencies of existential decision.

We believe that the understanding of history which we have presented here preserves a better balance between past, present, and future by remaining true to the myth of history in which event and interpretation arise together and stay together as succeeding generations enter into the "now" of the interpretative encounter with what has been created in the past. This is simply, in Vico's terms, the recognition that the historical nature of things—their ontology, if you wish—is nothing but their coming into being at certain times and in certain fashions. Moreover, as Vico and others have seen, and as the new hermeneutic has brought to our attention again, that which comes into being at certain times and in certain fashions, comes into being and is transmitted to us in terms of language. It is not only the interpretation but also the event itself which arises in terms of language, for, "rather than the saving event simply being described as it happened, to some extent it happened as it was described." [46] This linguistic unity is another way of pointing to the unity of event and interpretation. It is impossible to go "behind" this language, and this understanding of language enables us to be attentive to the yield of the past, and to recognize our dependence upon the community which has created this "yield" and transmitted it to us. Of course this is not to deny, as presumably is clear by this time, the importance of the "now" of personal appropriation. We must continually reappropriate the language-events of the past through that "ongoing linguistic transaction" in which events are "successively scored in ever-changing historical contexts." [47] Nevertheless, it is the original language-event which is successively scored—ultimately, the Yes, which is the word of all words.

6

Prospect for the Future

The implications and consequences for the Christian faith of all that we have referred to in the phrase "the myth of history" are profound and far-reaching. Now, while we have emphasized repeatedly the centrality of the original relational event of Jesus Christ, and while we would affirm that *it is that event* which we do apprehend, it is nevertheless clear that we do not apprehend that event in the same way in which it was originally apprehended. The critical difference is that we *self-consciously* apprehend it *as history*. The consequences of this, although we cannot yet see these clearly, are principally two: a new understanding of God, and a new understanding of the world. Let us look at each of these in turn.

If reality is understood as being historical in nature, and if we are not to conceive of God as existing somehow apart from the historical reality of our world, but as being in the closest relation to it, then we will affirm that God is to be understood as historical in nature. God brings reality into being, and what he brings into being is history, and we only know God through what he has made: history. "The true and the made are convertible." History does not give us some *additional* insight into God's "eternity." Rather, it is exactly our life within the myth of history which enables us to know God, and ourselves in relation to God. History is the structure of grace which constitutes the inclusive horizon of our theology. We do not want to say that at any particular point in history there is only one mode for "scoring" the gospel, but we do want to say that in our time history should become and is becoming the *normative* mode for the "scoring" of the gospel.

This new direction necessitates a continuous and thoroughgoing critique of the Hellenic mode of thought, which, in spite of nineteenth-century liberalism and everything else, still has a powerful influence upon the life and theology of the Church. (It is to be hoped that this critique will take place with the full recognition that at an earlier stage in the evolution of the Christian faith the Hellenic mode of thought was the appropriate mode for "scoring" the gospel.) The necessity of this critique should be evident from our preceding discussion. Thus, the emphasis which we have placed on hearing rather than seeing, on myth rather than man's self-sufficient reason, on the concrete and the novel rather than the ideal and the abiding, on the personal limiter rather than the normative limiter, and on the eschatological "golden age" of the future rather than the "golden age" which stands at the beginning of things—all bring our position into necessary and fundamental conflict with our Hellenic and classical heritage. Or, in short, when the myth of history is taken seriously, there will naturally be a challenging of, and opposition to, the Hellenic world-view since it does not share in that myth. As Justus Lawler has observed, "the hellenic *Denkform* (i.e., mindset) is by definition inimical to the only continuity modern man knows: the continuity of discontinuity." [1] The "continuity of discontinuity" is, from our point of view at least, the ceaseless waves of interpretation which break over us as, moving into an only partially known future, we find our existence caught up in the tension between promise and fulfillment. This, as Bernard Lonergan has observed, "cannot but run counter to classical expectations." [2]

One recent and vigorous critique of Hellenism has been

Leslie Dewart's, which it is instructive to examine in detail since, by a distinctively different path, he has arrived at a position that parallels that which we have been developing.[3] In *The Future of Belief,* he writes: "Christian theism may in the future conceive God as a historical presence, indeed as History, yet a history that would destroy neither human freedom nor God's reality precisely because such a God would not be eternal." [4] In language reminiscent of Fuchs's discussion of the present as "that presence which we share with one another," Dewart speaks of God as being "wholly present to all of man's and nature's time," and "that [God's] temporality consists in being *present to history*." [5] While this radically historical understanding of God stands in opposition to the Hellenic notion that there is a superbeing behind beings, or a supreme being who stands at the summit of the hierarchy of being,[6] it by no means follows, according to Dewart, that what men have left is a "make do" understanding of God to which they must for the time resign themselves. No, the God who is present to man in history is "God himself, in the fullness of his nature, for the Word of God that comes to man is *homoousios, consubstantialis Patri*." [7] In other words, the choices open to us are not exhausted by a Hellenically informed supernatural being, on the one hand, and the "death of God" on the other. If these were the only choices, then, Dewart implies, the "death of God" will prevail and, indeed, should prevail. There is a third alternative—one which Dewart advocates, and the one which we take to be consistent with the position which we have developed in the preceding chapters—namely, that God is the "reality beyond the totality of being [which] reveals itself by its *presence*." [8] When God is conceived of a historical presence, then the personal limiter, which we have argued is so essential to the historical understanding of reality, becomes the source of the controlling imagery for man's language about God. This parallel between our position and Dewart's becomes evident when, drawing upon Gabriel

Marcel, Dewart spells out the relationship which exists between the experience of human presence and the presence of
God.

. . . "When somebody's presence does really make itself felt
. . . it reveals me to myself, it makes me more fully myself than
I should be if I were not exposed to its impact." The reality of
human transcendence discloses the presence of a reality beyond
all actual and possible empirical intuition, *if* in the presence of
myself to myself I find that over and above my own agency (and
indeed as the ultimate condition of the possibility of that agency)
there is a presence which "reveals me to myself" in a super-
erogatory and gratuitous way, that is, by making me "more fully
myself than I should be if I were not exposed to its impact." [9]

This is the ecstatic confirmation of meaning, not because
there exists some supernatural reality that has somehow
been revealed to man, but because we have experienced
history as *grace*. History, in the full sense in which we have
defined it, is perceived as a "self-communicating and self-
giving superabundance," as a structure of grace which creates grace within us. It is out of this awareness that the
Christian expects the creation to support him, and which
leads him in thanksgiving to accept the moral obligation of
charity toward his fellow man.[10]

We have taken occasion to comment, mostly only in
passing, upon the relationship between the view of history
that we are developing and our attitude toward nature; as,
for example, the importance of the concept of evolution in
both history and nature, and the potentiality which a deepened perception of history holds for the renewal of sacramental worship. We also observed that included in the development of the historical understanding of reality was the
overcoming of the demonic in nature. The rule of the God
of history includes the realm of nature (cf. p. 23). Dewart
sees the relationship between nature and history in this same

light, and deems it an important reason for de-Hellenizing
the prevalent Christian view of the relationship. Rejecting
the traditional ambiguity of Christian theology and Western
thought generally toward nature, Dewart affirms that nature
like history is pervaded by grace.[11] He writes:

If a Christian looks at the world and understands nature through
hellenic eyes, he will find it necessary to assert the omnipotence
of God *over* and *against* nature. For in this view of nature,
either God is necessitated by it, or it is subject to God. But in
the contemporary experience nature is no longer understood as
the principle which necessitates from within the operations of
beings, and therefore makes them resist violence from without.
We do not see nature as the source of independence and self-
sufficiency which it was for Aristotle. Therefore, God does not
have power *over* nature. The reason is that nature does not as
such resist him.[12]

We would agree with this statement of Dewart's, but only
after qualifications that may well be unacceptable to him.
The difficulty with his proposition that God does not have
power *over* nature is that in the struggle of the prophets
against the baalim of Canaan, in the so-called nature miracles in the Gospels, as well as in Paul's statements about
the "principalities and powers," it *is* scripturally affirmed
that God is sovereign *over* nature, or, at least, over a very
real aspect of nature, the demonic.* With respect to this
scriptural affirmation, one must make two observations immediately: (1) that the biblical point of view does not conceive the demonic, or its "source," in a Hellenic context of
a rationally conceived hierarchy of being; (2) that in biblical thought the demonic is seen as a nonrational and evil
resistance to the rule of God. With these observations in
mind, one can qualify Dewart's proposition thus: It is not
nature *as such* which resists God, but the nonrational de-

* It might be argued that Paul is tainted with Hellenism, but this
cannot be said of the Synoptic Gospels and the statements of the
prophets.

monic power which erupts in nature (and in history) in the
course of the historical-evolutionary—or, more traditionally,
eschatological—process when the rule of God is incom-
pletely realized or effective. In other words, when the rule of
God prevails, then the demonic, the nonrational, is eliminated, and nature is brought into its authentic, theonomous
state. Moreover, with the coming of Christ, the reign of God
does prevail over the demonic in nature. Consequently, the
theonomous situation is present in nature, although the perfection of this "new creation" remains to be worked out in
the historical-evolutionary process.[13]

Far from weakening Dewart's proposition, these qualifications, we believe, render his total position more consistent.
If nature, like man, is to be pulled right into history, and if
man and nature have a profound relationship to one another
within the context of history, then it is eminently consistent
that nature should share in the "fall" and that man and
nature should go forward together into a creation which is
new for both.

Having made these qualifications, we would go on emphatically to assent to Dewart's contention that in the alternative that he has proposed to the Hellenic way of viewing
God and the world,

grace continues to be what Christian belief always held it was,
but nature ceases in every way to be opposed to grace: [like man]
it is naturally apt to receive grace, because that is how it was in
fact created. Since nature is essentially contingent, deriving its
intelligibility from its factuality and historicity, nature is historically, not metaphysically, related to grace. Grace is thus
understood as a historical fact, God's presence to man, which
existentially qualifies the historical intelligibility of nature in a
definitive way.[14]

What Dewart says here about grace we would understand to
apply equally—for indeed they are the same—to the christologically based myth of history. In fact, he catches up *in
nuce* most of the major themes of our preceding chapters

when he goes on to elaborate in a brilliant, highly condensed statement his "credo" concerning grace:

Grace transmutes mere spatio-temporal *facts* into ultimate, religious *truths;* it transposes, as it were, abstract point-events into three-dimensional, real-life happenings in their full ontic reality. The difference between a "natural" and a "supernatural" event or reality (or between the "secular" and the "religious" explanations thereof), concerning any order whatever of reality, from the amoeba to the ziggurat . . . is not in the abstract spatio-temporal *content* but in the existential historical *form* of the event or reality (or of the ascertained explanation thereof). Hence, a non-religious order of either everyday experience or scientific explanation lacks faith, professes to have the rigor of black and white and, wishing to be absolute and self-suffi-cient, excludes revelation. Christian experience, whether com-mon-sense or scientific, on the other hand, is colored by faith. It imports belief into knowledge, not to judge it but to interpret it in relation to existence; not in order to argue *a priori* what is and what is not true, or even what might and might not be true, but in order to discover the inner meaning, or the fuller sense, of the one and only "natural" truth. In this sense, too, it would not be inexact—though, to repeat, somewhat equivocal and misleading—to say that Christian speculation and Christian everyday experience are becoming naturalistic and secular.[15]

This is a historical and theonomous view of reality; here in Tillich's fine phrase, "Religion is the substance of culture, culture is the form of religion." [16] Here man and nature are united in a historical and evolutionary process of grace. Here the world is totally open to God. This means, both, that "in God nature can do *anything*," and that the world is "totally open to *future creation by man*." [17] These two proc-esses are really one, and both manifest the power of the word of God to recreate the world. In history, word of God and word of man are joined in a mutual presence to one another "in the *conscious* creation of the world." [18] Here the "mutuality" must be stressed, "for man indeed makes his-tory, but history is not reducible to what man freely makes

of it. History is made by man but in the presence of God.
. . . *With* God indeed all things, all history, is possible to
man." [19]

When history is understood in this way, it is understood
as myth; and when we understand history as myth, we
receive it as grace. The implications of this understanding
for the Christian faith are enormously exciting. Moreover,
as hopefully our study has made clear, these implications
are already beginning to be recognized and explored on all
sides. Let us focus briefly upon a few of these implications.

We have had occasion to speak of how the myth of history gives us a new entrance into sacramental worship, and
we have had a great deal to say about what takes place in
the hearing of the word of God. We have noted that language and event which cannot be separated. This is what
man makes in history; and in making language in prayer,
and in all of his speaking, man knows himself to be in the
presence of God, and thus knows himself and his world.[20]

This is how the matter stands *within* the myth of history;
this situation is objectively true (we omit the quotation
marks) *within* the myth of history. There are other objective
truths arising out of other religions and world-views. Many
Christians (leaving others aside) find these alternative possibilities of objectivity intolerable, and in the name of "fact"
seek to destroy all objectivities but their own. This is offen-
sive in the extreme, not so much because it lacks "open-
mindedness," but because it is largely blind to grace other
than its own; and, even more, because it is unfaithful to the
grace of the myth of history which knows nothing of "facts"
which are at man's disposal, and upon which he may construct polemics—and hence be independent of grace!

In contrast to this, the objectivity upon which we as
Christians may depend is that for which we have made our
decision, and out of which we may freely witness to all
others—the objectivity which arises out of our participation
in the christologically based myth of history. As a result of
the arising of the modern historical consciousness, we are

coming to recognize much more clearly than before the peculiar quality of our mythic objectivity; a quality which distinguishes it from all other mythic objectivities. This quality is the evolutionary, or process, character of Christian truth. This process is marked both by its not being a process toward a *restitutio in integrum* but toward a *"new creation,"* and by the fact man plays a constitutive part in this process. The clear recognition of this evolutionary and humane quality of the Christian faith opens possibilities for ending the sequestration of religion from culture, which has been going on since the late medieval period, and of working toward a reconstitution of the fragmented elements of our Western (and increasingly, world) civilization.

This reconstitution is being called for on all sides. Thus, Jürgen Moltmann, in his *Theology of Hope,* calls for an end of the "dual track in the history of modern thought," which splits experience into, on the one hand, "the methodizing approach to world experience," and, on the other hand, the "ineffable, solitary subjectivity, which must flee all contact with reality and all concessions toward it in order to abide by itself." [21] This is, of course, precisely the unloving dualism which we have discussed in its various forms, but which is perhaps manifested most clearly in the dichotomy between *Historie/Geschichte.* Although Moltmann's approach to this problem is by a route quite different from our own, his pointing out of the way forward is remarkably similar to our own.

Theology will have to take the hardened antitheses and make them fluid once more, to mediate in the contradiction between them and reconcile them. That, however, is only possible when the category of history . . . is rediscovered in such a way that it does not deny the antithesis [*Historie/Geschichte*] in question, but spans it and understands it as an element in an advancing process.[22]

This is precisely what we have attempted to do in terms of the myth of history which brings the sacred and the profane together in loving union, but without denying the distinction between them. In such an erotics of history, history is understood as a *Gestalt* of grace which delivers man from the terror that binds him when history is experienced only as being "profane," but which, at the same time, does not place man in a new bondage to the sacred.[23]

It is along these lines that our civilization strives to overcome the dichotomy between the sacred and the profane. This striving, as should be clear from the preceding chapters, is remarkable in the diversity of its expression. This striving is also remarkable in that it has taken so long to develop. We share the amazement that Owen Barfield expresses when he writes:

I believe that the blind-spot which posterity will find most startling in the last hundred years or so of Western civilization, is, that it had, on the one hand, a religion which differed from all others in its acceptance of time, and of a particular point in time, as a cardinal element in its faith; that it had, on the other hand, a picture in its mind of the history of the earth and man as an evolutionary process; and that it neither saw nor supposed any connection whatever between the two.[24]

This separation is being overcome, and this is itself part of the evolutionary process. As in all evolutionary processes, however, this means genuine change. For the Christian faith the change means the recognition of God within the substance of history; and this change brings with it a new apprehension of the future-directed, eschatological nature of history and Christian faith. God is continually coming to new expression in the worship, prayer, theology, and action of the Church in its widest sense. Our objective truth is found in the truth of the endless waves of interpretation which break over us. This is the only kind of objective truth possible for those who live within the christologically based myth of history; for were we ever to arrive once and for all at such truth, then the tension between promise and fulfillment would be broken, and the sacral power of history, the power of God's reign in history, would be destroyed. History is, in Kierkegaard's terms, a "passion for what is possible" [25] as history moves toward, but never reaches, its fulfillment; but this is only so because history is also a passion for the promise of Jesus Christ which brings the possibilities of history into being.[26]

The political implications for our civilization of this understanding of history are evident, and it is one of the valuable contributions of the theology of hope that it has started the process of focusing and developing these implications for us.[27] The man who lives within what we have called the myth of history is kept "*in stata viatoris,* in that unresolved openness to world questions," [28] and consequently committed to "the realization of righteousness, freedom and humanity here in the light of the promised future that is to come." [29] "Whenever that happens, Christianity embraces its true nature and becomes a witness to the future of Christ." [30]

Now the suggestion is being made with increasing frequency that this "future," this "passion for the future," which is so much a part of historical expression, be drawn upon for our imagery of God; and that the traditional space-related imagery (the God who is "up there" or "out there" or "in the depths") be omitted altogether. This would be to draw *directly* upon the myth of history for our language about God, both in his immanence and in his transcendence. The immanence of God is manifested through what God and man have made in the course of their historical experience in past and present. The transcendence of God is also manifested in the very substance of historical experience; for, as we have seen, historical experience, while attentive to and guided by the past, continually runs into the future in the ever new creation of meaning and the consequent establishment of the ontology of the world. It is this evolution toward fullness and perfection, the advance to the Omega Point, which is seen within the myth of history as being the manifestation of the transcendence of God. The transcendent God is not up, out, or down, but in the future. In a review of contemporary theological trends, George Lindbeck observes that the specifically modern experience of that

which transcends the reality which we experience and know is no longer thought of (as it was in a two-story, non-historical universe) as a realm of timeless truth, value and being above us (or, where the immanence of the divine is emphasized, within and at the ground of being) which supplies the perfectly stable structures of life. Rather, that which transcends the world of our experience lies ahead, in the decipherable possibilities for good and evil into which we find ourselves hurled with ever increasing speed. Our contemporaries are not likely to encounter transcendence as something discontinuous with the world, as something which is to be entered by escaping out of time into eternity. Rather, they meet it as *the future which is continuous, yet radically different,* from our present world; they encounter it within the reality of their experience as the anticipation or projections of the coming world.[31]

The phrase "continuous, yet radically different" points to the continuity or inseparability of God's transcendence and his immanence. Nor is one any less a matter of faith than the other, for both are dependent upon the original relational event, Jesus Christ, which establishes the myth of history. It is this event that incorporates man into the divine-human history running out of the past into the future, enabling the word of man to be also the word of God, for: "In one man the inwardness of the Divine Name had been fully realized; the final participation, whereby man's Creator speaks from within man himself, had been accomplished. The Word had been made flesh." [32]

Author's Notes

INTRODUCTION

1. Van A. Harvey, *The Historian and the Believer* (New York: Macmillan, 1966), p. 4.

2. Mircea Eliade, *The Myth of the Eternal Return* (New York: Pantheon, 1954), p. 153. Italics added.

3. Cf. *ibid.*

4. *Ibid.*

5. Cf. *ibid.*, pp. 159ff. *et passim.*

6. Cf. Paul M. van Buren, *The Secular Meaning of the Gospel* (London: SCM, 1963), p. 155 *et passim.*

7. Gordon D. Kaufman, "On the Meaning of 'God': Transcendence without Mythology," *Harvard Theological Review* (April, 1966). Reprinted in *New Theology No. 4*, Marty and Peerman, eds. (New York: Macmillan, 1967), p. 72. Kaufman's italics.

8. Rudolf Bultmann, *History and Eschatology* (Edinburgh: University Press, 1957), p. 153.

9. The terminology of "original participation" and "final participation" is drawn from Owen Barfield's brilliant book, *Saving the Appearances: A Study in Idolatry* (New York: Harcourt, Brace and World, n.d.).

10. Cf. Joseph Sittler, "The Principal Problem for Protestant Theology Today," *The Word in History*, T. Patrick Burke, ed. (New York: Sheed and Ward, 1966), pp. 60-68.

11. Jürgen Moltmann, *Theology of Hope*, trans. James W. Leitch (London: SCM, 1967), p. 16.

Chapter 1: HISTORY AS A FORM OF MYTH

1. Cf. Mircea Eliade, *The Myth of the Eternal Return* (New York: Pantheon, 1954).

2. Giambattista Vico, *The New Science*, trans. T. G. Bergin and M. H. Fisch (Ithaca: Cornell University Press, 1948), par. 147.

Cf. Walter J. Ong, S.J., *The Presence of the Word* (New Haven: Yale University Press, 1967), p. 227.

3. This situation is reflected, for example, in the selections found in the comprehensive anthology, *Theories of History* (Glencoe: Free Press, 1959), Patrick Gardiner, ed.

4. For some pertinent and discerning observations on the limitations of pragmatism see Michael Novak, "What Is Theology's Standpoint?" *Theology Today*, XXV, No. 1, 37-51.

5. Cf. Barbara Tuchman, *New York Times Book Review*, March 8, 1964, p. 1.

6. Ong, *op. cit.*, p. 228.

7. Cf. Chap. II, *infra*.

8. Mircea Eliade, *Myth and Reality* (London: Allen and Unwin, 1964), pp. 18f.

9. *Ibid.*, p. 18.

10. *Ibid.*, p. 18. Eliade's italics.

11. *Ibid.*

12. *Ibid.*

13. *Ibid.*, p. 19.

14. Cf. Gerhard von Rad, *Old Testament Theology* (New York: Harper & Row, 1965), II, pp. 107ff. *et passim;* Walther Eichrodt, *Theology of the Old Testament* (London: SCM, 1961); Werner G. Kümmel, *Promise and Fulfilment* (3rd ed.; London: SCM, 1957).

15. James D. Smart, *The Interpretation of Scripture* (London: SCM, 1961), p. 102.

16. Cf. James Barr, "Revelation through History in the Old Testament and in Modern Theology," *Interpretation*, XVII, No. 2 (April, 1963), 193-205.

17. Dietrich Bonhoeffer, *Creation and Fall* (London: SCM, 1959), p. 22.

18. Walther Eichrodt, *Theology of the Old Testament*, I, p. 491.

19. Cf. *Ibid.*, pp. 468-469.

20. *Ibid.*, p. 486.

21. George Ernest Wright, "History and Reality," in *The Old Testament and Christian Faith*, Bernhard W. Anderson, ed. (New York: Harper & Row, 1963), p. 195.

22. Karl Barth, *Christengemeinde und Buergergemeinde*, 1946, p. 36. Quoted by W. Dantine, *Scottish Journal of Theology*, XVIII (June, 1965), 133.

23. Owen Barfield, *Saving the Appearances: A Study in Idolatry* (New York: Harcourt, Brace & World, n.d.), pp. 169-170.

24. Cf. Friedrich Gogarten, *Demythologizing and History*, trans. N. H. Smith (London: SCM, 1955), Chap. VIII. One wonders, since the awareness of sin is simultaneously the awareness of grace, why Gogarten's emphasis here falls so heavily on sin. This necessitates a correspondingly heavy emphasis upon the redemption from

sin, and this obscures the positive aspect of man's awareness of his responsibility for history, namely, his awareness of his lordship over God's blessed earth.

25. Martin Buber, *I and Thou*, trans. Ronald Gregor Smith (2nd. ed.; New York: Charles Scribner's Sons, 1958), p. 54. Cf. Gordon Kaufman, "On the Meaning of 'Act of God'," *The Harvard Theological Review*, 61, No. 2 (April, 1968), 175-201. Kaufman's brilliant and lucid article presents a position which we interpret as being essentially compatible with Buber's position, and with our own. Kaufman's "master act of God" corresponds to our "myth of history."

26. Martin Buber, *Moses: The Revelation and the Covenant* (New York: Harper & Row, 1958), p. 18.

27. Buber, *I and Thou*, p. 11.

28. *Ibid.*, p. 4.

29. *Ibid.*, p. 54.

30. *Ibid.*

31. For a discussion of these inconsistencies see my "I-Thou and I-It: An Attempted Clarification of their Relationship," *Journal of Religion*, XLIII, No. 3 (July, 1963), 193-209.

32. Cf. R. G. Collingwood, *The Idea of History* (Oxford: Oxford University Press, 1946), p. 315.

33. Cf. Heinrich Ott, "The Historical Jesus and the Ontology of History," in *The Historical Jesus and the Kerygmatic Christ*, Carl E. Braaten and Roy A. Harrisville, eds. (Nashville: Abingdon Press, 1964), p. 163.

Chapter 2: *GIAMBATTISTA VICO AND THE MODERN HISTORICAL CONSCIOUSNESS*

1. Cf. Collingwood, *op. cit.*, pp. 46ff.

2. Cf. M. H. Fisch and T. G. Bergin (eds.), *The Autobiography of Giambattista Vico* (Ithaca: Cornell University Press, 1944), pp. 20-60 of the "Introduction."

3. Heinz Zahrnt, *The Historical Jesus*, trans. J. S. Bowden (New York: Harper & Row, 1963), p. 24.

4. Cf. Paul M. van Buren, *The Secular Meaning of the Gospel* (London: SCM, 1963), pp. xiii-xiv, 193ff. *et passim*.

5. Cf. Arnold E. Loen, *Secularization: Science without God?*, trans. Margaret Kohl (London: SCM, 1967), Chap. 4 *et passim*.

6. Cf. *ibid.*, p. 116.

7. Collingwood, *op. cit.*, p. 65. Cf. Robert Flin, *Vico* (London: William Blackwood, 1894), esp. Chaps. 5-8.

8. Cf. Gardiner, *op. cit.*, p. 12.

9. *The New Science of Giambattista Vico*, translated from the third edition (1744) by T. G. Bergin and M. H. Fisch (Ithaca:

Cornell University Press, 1948). All references to *The New Science* itself will be given in terms of paragraph (par.) numbers. These numbers are uniform with those in the text edited by Fausto Nicolini and appearing as Vol. 112 and part of Vol. 113 in *Scritteri d'Italia* (Bari, 1928). In a few instances our quotations from *The New Science* have been slightly modified in the light of the slightly modified translation of *The New Science* found in Fisch and Bergin's *The New Science of Giambattista Vico* (New York: Doubleday, 1961). This is an abridged and revised edition of Fisch and Bergin's earlier edition of 1948. Paragraph numbers are uniform in the two editions.

10. Cf. Isaiah Berlin, "The Philosophical Ideas of Giambattista Vico," in *Art and Ideas in Eighteenth Century Italy* (Rome: Edizioni di Storia e Letteratura, 1960), p. 176.

11. Cf. James Brown, *Subject and Object in Modern Theology* (London: SCM, 1955), Chap. 1. Our discussion in this area is also indebted to Berlin, *op. cit.*, pp. 162ff. *et passim*.

12. Quoted by Frederick Copleston, *A History of Philosophy* (Westminster: Newman Press, 1960), IV, pp. 97-98.

13. Quoted by Copleston, *op. cit.*, p. 100.

14. Berlin, *op. cit.*, p. 163.

15. Cf. *The New Science*, par. 85.

16. Cf. Berlin, *op. cit.*, p. 165. The phrase *verum et factum convertuntur* is apparently Vico's own reworking of such well-known "tags" as *verum et bonum convertuntur* (e.g., *Summa Theologica*, 1:16:4) and *ens et verum convertuntur* (e.g., *Summa Theologica*, 1:16:3). Cf. also Flint, *op. cit.*, p. 93; Fisch and Bergin, "Introduction" to *The Autobiography of Giambattista Vico*, pp. 38ff.; A. Robert Caponigri, *Time and Idea: The Theory of History in Giambattista Vico* (London: Routledge and Kegan Paul, 1953), pp. 155f.

17. Berlin, *op. cit.*, p. 165. Cf. Max Scheler, *On the Eternal in Man*, trans. Bernard Noble (London: SCM, 1960), p. 390.

18. Berlin, *op. cit.*, p. 169. Used with permission.

19. Cf. *The New Science*, par. 349.

20. Cf. *Ibid.*, pars. 331, 349.

21. Cf. Caponigri, *op. cit.*, pp. 148ff.

22. Berlin, *op. cit.*, p. 177.

23. Caponigri, *op. cit.*, p. 149. Cf. Berlin, *op. cit.*, p. 196.

24. Berlin, *op. cit.*, p. 173.

25. *The New Science*, par. 147.

26. Caponigri, *op. cit.*, pp. 170-171. Cf. Susan Sontag, *Against Interpretation* (New York: Dell, 1961), Chap. 1.

27. Caponigri, *op. cit.*, pp. 176-177.

28. *Ibid.*, p. 172. Cf. our discussion of Buber, Chap. I *supra*.

29. Cf. Berlin, *op. cit.*, p. 203.

30. Cf. *ibid.*, p. 216.

31. *The New Science*, pars. 34, 496.

32. *Ibid.*, par. 118.
33. Cf. *ibid.*, par. 209.
34. *Ibid.*, par. 34.
35. *Ibid.*, par. 403.
36. Cf. *ibid.*, par. 210. Cf. also par. 403.
37. *Ibid.*, par. 401.
38. *Ibid.*, par. 403.
39. *Ibid.*, par. 34. Cf. *The New Science*, pars. 32, 225, 401.
40. *The New Science*, par. 484.
41. Cf. *ibid.*, pars. 484, 433.
42. Paul Tillich, *Dynamics of Faith* (New York: Harper & Row 1958), p. 42.
43. *The New Science*, par. 408.
44. Caponigri, *op. cit.*, pp. 166-167.
45. Quoted by Berlin, *op. cit.*, p. 183.
46. *The New Science*, par. 7.
47. *Ibid.*, par. 314.
48. Cf. Caponigri, *op. cit.*, p. 155 *et passim*.
49. Collingwood, *op. cit.*, p. 65. For other discussions of this aspect of Vico's thought, see Caponigri, *op. cit.*, esp. p. 107; and Benedetto Croce, *The Philosophy of Giambattista Vico*, trans. R. G. Collingwood (London: Allen and Unwin, 1913), esp. p. 116.
50. Cf. Berlin, *op. cit.*, pp. 214ff.
51. Cf. *ibid.*, p. 227.
52. Cf. *The New Science*, pars. 165ff.
53. Cf. e.g., *ibid.*, par 557.
54. Cf. Kenneth Hamilton, *Revolt against Heaven* (Grand Rapids: Eerdmans, 1965), Chap. IV.
55. Gerhard Ebeling, *Wort und Glaube* (Tübingen: J. C. B. Mohr, 1960), p. 343. Quoted by Schubert M. Ogden, "What Sense Does It Make to Say, 'God Acts in History'?" *Journal of Religion,* XLIII (January, 1963), 19.
56. Leslie Dewart, *The Future of Belief* (New York: Herder and Herder, 1966), p.198.

Chapter 3: TOWARD A POST-CARTESIAN VIEW OF HISTORY: THE QUEST OF THE HISTORICAL JESUS AND THE THEOLOGY OF RUDOLF BULTMANN

1. A recent, readable review is Heinz Zahrnt's *The Historical Jesus,* trans. J. S. Bowden (New York: Harper & Row, 1963), esp. pp. 17-54. Cf. Norman Perrin, *Rediscovering the Teaching of Jesus* (New York: Harper & Row, 1967), Chap. V. This chapter includes a good, brief critical review of the historical-Jesus movement. Perrin sees the movement as beginning with H. S. Reimarus (1694-1768), a contemporary of Vico.
2. A survey of the influence of Vico upon European intellectual

history may be found in Berlin, *op. cit., passim;* and in the "Introduction" to M. H. Fisch and T. G. Bergin's translation of *The Autobiography of Giambattista Vico* (Ithaca: Cornell University Press, 1944).

3. Cf. Collingwood, *op. cit.,* pp. 76ff., 143ff. *et passim.*

4. Van A. Harvey, *The Historian and the Believer* (New York: Macmillan, 1966), p. 4.

5. Zahrnt, *op. cit.,* p. 54.

6. Rudolf Bultmann, *Glauben und Verstehen* (Tübingen, 1933), I, p. 2.

7. Cf. James M. Robinson, *A New Quest of the Historical Jesus* (London: SCM, 1959), pp. 26f.

8. Cf. Ebeling, *Word and Faith* (Philadelphia: Fortress Press, 1963), p. 290.

9. D. M. Baillie, *God Was in Christ* (New York: Charles Scribner's Sons, 1948), p. 52.

10. Perrin, *op. cit.,* p. 212.

11. Cf. Harvey, *op. cit.,* p. 10.

12. Cf. Mircea Eliade, *Myth and Reality* (New York: Harper & Row, 1963), pp. 162ff.

13. Zahrnt, *op. cit.,* pp. 48-49. Used with permission. Cf. Perrin, *op. cit.,* pp. 215f.

14. Cf. Robinson, *op. cit.,* pp. 32ff.

15. Cf. Zahrnt, *op. cit.,* p. 50.

16. Cf. Martin Kähler, *The So-Called Historical Jesus and the Historic, Biblical Christ,* trans. C. E. Braaten (Philadelphia: Fortress Press, 1964), pp. 51ff. *et passim.*

17. Cf. Perrin, *op. cit.,* p. 215.

18. Rudolf Bultmann, "New Testament and Mythology," in Hans Werner Bartsch (ed.), *Kerygma and Myth,* I, trans. R. H. Fuller (London: SPCK, 1957), pp. 1-44.

19. Cf. for example, Schubert Ogden, *Christ without Myth* (New York: Harper & Row, 1961), esp. Chap. III; John B. Cobb, Jr., *Living Options in Protestant Theology* (Philadelphia: Westminster Press, 1962), Chap. 9; P. Joseph Cahill, S.J., "Rudolf Bultmann and Post-Bultmann Tendencies," *Catholic Biblical Quarterly* (April, 1964), and reprinted in *New Theology No. 2* (New York: Macmillan, 1965), pp. 222-254. The agreement among these various critics is extensive, although, of course, not complete.

20. Cf. Carl E. Braaten's "Introduction" to Martin Kähler's *The So-Called Historical Jesus and the Historic, Biblical Christ,* pp. 21f. Cf. also Julius Schniewind, "A Reply to Bultmann," *Kerygma and Myth,* I, p. 82.

21. Cf. Rudolf Bultmann, *Jesus Christ and Mythology* (London: SCM, 1960), p. 85. Cf. also Bultmann, "New Testament and Mythology," p. 43 *et passim.*

22. Cf. H. Richard Niebuhr, *The Meaning of Revelation* (New York: Macmillan, 1941), esp. Chap. II.

23. Cf. Rudolf Bultmann, *Essays: Philosophical and Theological,* trans. J. C. G. Grieg (New York: Macmillan, 1955), pp. 257f. (hereafter referred to as *Essays*). Cf. also Ogden, *op. cit.,* pp. 88f.

24. In our discussion it will be necessary from time to time to use the German terms *Historie* and *Geschichte* because of the difficulty and clumsiness in making this distinction in English. This difficulty is also present in regard to adjectival forms of these terms, namely *historisch* and *geschichtlich*. Their more or less commonly accepted translation as, respectively, "historical" and "historic," does little to convey the distinction which is effected by the German terminology.

25. Rudolf Bultmann, "A Reply to the Theses of J. Schniewind," *Kerygma and Myth,* I, p. 117.

26. Rudolf Bultmann, *Existence and Faith: Shorter Writings of Rudolf Bultmann,* Schubert M. Ogden, ed. and trans. (New York: Meridian, 1960), p. 294. Used with permission. (Hereafter referred to as *Existence and Faith*.) Italics added. Whether scientific knowledge may be understood strictly in terms of the subject-object scheme is a controversial matter which we will let pass.

27. Bultmann, *Existence and Faith,* p. 291. Bultmann's italics.

28. *Ibid.,* pp. 291-292. Used with permission.

29. Cf. *ibid.,* p. 292. Cf. also Bultmann, *Essays,* p. 241, n. 1.

30. Cf. Paul Ricoeur, *The Symbolism of Evil,* trans. Emerson Buchanan (New York: Harper & Row, 1967), p. 357 *et passim*.

31. Cf. Bultmann, *Existence and Faith,* pp. 292ff.

32. *Ibid.,* p. 292.

33. *Ibid.,* p. 293.

34. *Ibid.*

35. *Ibid.,* p. 294.

36. Bultmann, *Essays,* p. 243.

37. Cf. Harvey, *op. cit.,* Chap. VII.

38. Cf. *ibid.,* p. 213. Cf. Bultmann, *History and Eschatology,* p. 121, *et. passim*.

39. Harvey, *op. cit.,* pp. 213-214.

40. Bultmann, *History and Eschatology* (Edinburgh: University Press, 1957), p. 122.

41. Bultmann, *History and Eschatology,* p. 142.

42. Bultmann, *Existence and Faith,* p. 294.

43. Bultmann, *History and Eschatology,* p. 141.

44. *Ibid.,* p. 144.

45. *Ibid.,* p. 145. Bultmann's italics.

46. Cf. Bultmann; *Essays,* pp. 188f., 254.

47. Cf. Bultmann, *Essays,* p. 246. Bultmann's italics.

48. *Ibid.*

49. *Ibid.,* Bultmann's italics.

50. One red herring which is perhaps worth a note at this point: Does not the thoroughly existential understanding of history proposed here exclude the historical study of natural phenomena, e.g., climate or agriculture in eighteenth-century England? Not at all, for such a study would be concerned with the economic and physical reactions of eighteenth-century Englishmen as to their climatic and agricultural situation; otherwise it is not history, but meterology or agronomy.

51. Cf. Bultmann, *History and Eschatology*. Chap. X *et passim*.

52. Buber, *I and Thou*, p. 54.

53. Bultmann, *History and Eschatology*, p. 152.

54. Cf. *ibid.*, p. 121.

55. Bultmann, *History and Eschatology*, p. 150. Bultmann acknowledges a "relative freedom" which operates even when one is determined by the past, but this is not adequate for historical existence.

56. *Ibid.*, p. 16. Consequently "history" and "historian" had a radically different meaning for the Greeks than that which they have for us.

57. *Ibid.*, p. 151.

58. *Ibid.*, p. 150.

59. *Ibid.*, p. 152.

60. Cf. *ibid.*, pp. 121, 155.

61. Bultmann, *History and Eschatology*, p. 149. Italics added. Cf. *History and Eschatology*, Chap. VII.

62. Bultmann, *Essays*, p. 286.

63. Bultmann, "New Testament and Mythology" quoted by Ogden, *Christ without Myth*, p. 83.

64. Bultmann, *History and Eschatology*, p. 153.

65. Cf. Ogden, *op. cit.*, pp. 81ff.

66. Ogden, *op. cit.*, p. 83. Ogden's italics.

67. Ogden, *op. cit.*, p. 83.

68. *Ibid.*, p. 154.

69. Rudolf Bultmann, "Bultmann Replies to His Critics," *Kerygma and Myth*, I, pp. 210-211. Cf. Ogden, *op. cit.*, p. 145. Cf. also Cahill, *op. cit.*, p. 237.

70. Cf. W. Taylor Stevenson, "I-Thou and I-It: An Attempted Clarification of Their Relationship," *Journal of Religion*, XLIII (July, 1964), pp. 193-209.

71. P. Joseph Cahill, "Bultmann and Post-Bultmann Tendencies," *New Theology No. 2* (New York: Macmillan, 1965), pp. 242-243. Used with permission.

72. H. W. Bartsch (ed.), *Kerygma und Mythos*, Vol. I (2nd ed.; Hamburg: Herbert Reich-Evangelischer Verlag, 1951), p. 22, n. 2. Quoted by Ogden, *op. cit.*, p. 25.

73. Bultmann, "Bultmann Replies to His Critics," p. 210.

74. Cf. Schubert M. Ogden, "The Significance of Rudolf Bultmann for Contemporary Theology," in *The Theology of Rudolf Bultmann,* p. 113.

75. Cf. Bultmann, "New Testament and Mythology," p. 11.

76. Cf. *ibid.,* pp. 17ff. *et passim.* Cf. Ogden, *Christ Without Myth,* pp. 76ff.

77. Bultmann's views are so well known, and recent detailed expositions of his thought in this area are so readily available, that further description of his position on our part seems unnecessary. See, for example, Schubert Ogden's excellent exposition in *Christ without Myth,* esp. Chap. II.

78. Cf. Ogden, *Christ without Myth,* pp. 28ff., 76ff. *et passim.*

79. Bultmann, "A Reply to the Theses of J. Schniewind," p. 103.

80. The nineteenth-century liberal, as we have observed, *believed* himself to be working with strictly objective history, but in fact he consistently laced his objectivity with nineteenth-century humanism. Contemporary fundamentalists *believe* that their acceptance of the straightforward objectivity of biblical myth is the sole presupposition of their exegesis, and are unaware of its heavy debt to positivism.

81. Cf. Bultmann, "A Reply to the Theses of J. Schniewind," pp. 104-105, for example. Cf. also Ogden, *Christ without Myth,* p. 77.

82. Bultmann, *op. cit.,* p. 104.

83. Cf. Ogden, *op. cit.,* pp. 28ff., 76ff. *et passim.*

84. Cf. Ogden, *op. cit.,* p. 201.

85. Cf. Edwin M. Good, "The Meaning of Demythologization," in *The Theology of Rudolf Bultmann,* p. 35f. Good's comments on Bultmann's treatment of myth move in the same area as our own.

86. Bultmann, "New Testament and Mythology," pp. 10-11. Italics added.

87. *Ibid.,* p. 11.

88. *Ibid.,* p. 16.

89. Bultmann, "A Reply to the Theses of J. Schniewind," *Kerygma and Myth,* I, pp. 102ff.

90. Bultmann, "New Testament and Mythology," p. 10.

91. Bultmann, *History and Eschatology,* p. 151. Bultmann's italics.

92. Paul Ricoeur, *The Symbolism of Evil,* p. 352.

93. *Ibid.;* p. 350.

94. *Ibid.,* p. 349.

Chapter 4: TOWARD AN EROTICS OF HISTORY: LANGUAGE AND HISTORY

1. Sontag, *op. cit.,* p. 14.

2. *Ibid.,* p. 5.

3. Cf. *ibid.*, p. 4.
4. *Ibid.*, p. 13.
5. *Ibid.*
6. *Ibid.*, p. 14. Sontag's italics.
7. Buber, *I and Thou*, p. 11.
8. *Ibid.*, Buber's italics.
9. *Ibid.*, p. 4. Italics added.
10. *Ibid.*, p. 39.
11. *Ibid.*, p. 11.
12. *Ibid.*, p. 110.
13. *Ibid.*
14. Cf. Vico, *The New Science*, pars. 34 and 496.
15. Cf. *ibid.*, pars. 32, 401.
16. *Ibid.*, par. 147.
17. Vico, *Ancient Wisdom of the Italians*, quoted by Berlin, *op. cit.*, p. 183.
18. Gerhard Ebeling, *Word and Faith*, trans. James W. Leitch (Philadelphia: Fortress Press, 1963), p. 318. Ebeling's italics.
19. James M. Robinson, "Hermeneutic since Barth," in *The New Hermeneutic*, James M. Robinson and John B. Cobb, Jr., eds. (New York: Harper & Row, 1964), p. 6. Cf. also pp. 39, 46ff. *et passim.*
20. Cf. James M. Robinson, *A New Quest of the Historical Jesus* (London: SCM, 1959), Chap. II.
21. Hans-Georg Gadamer, *Wahrbeit und Methode: Grundzuge einer philosophischen Hermeneutik* (Tübingen: J. C. B. Mohr, 1960), p. 261. Quoted by Robinson, *The New Hermeneutic*, p. 70.
22. Cf. Buber, *I and Thou*, p. 11: ". . . man takes his stand in speech and talks from there."
23. Cf. *The Later Heidegger and Theology*, James M. Robinson and John B. Cobb, Jr., eds. (New York: Harper & Row, 1963), esp. Robinson's essay "The German Discussion of the Later Heidegger," pp. 3-76. Our somewhat selective exposition of Heidegger focuses upon his later thought, i.e., during and after World War II. Our decision to concentrate upon this later phase arises out of the judgment that it is this later thought which helps show the way out of the problem in regard to history which emerged in our discussion of Bultmann. We would agree with John Macquarrie and others that the distinction between the earlier and later Heidegger should not be overstressed. Cf. John Macquarrie, "Heidegger: Early and Later," *Anglican Theological Review*, XLIX (January, 1967), 3-16.
24. Cf. John Macquarrie, *Studies in Christian Existentialism* (London: SCM, 1965), p. 46.
25. Heidegger sees this intellectual tradition as extending back beyond Descartes all the way to Plato; but a comprehensive state-

ment of Heidegger's position in this matter would take us far beyond the scope of our book.

26. Martin Heidegger, *Essays in Metaphysics: Identity and Difference*, trans. Kurt F. Leidecher (New York: Philosophical Library, 1960), p. 32. Italics added.

27. *Ibid.*, p. 65.

28. Robinson, "The German Discussion of the Later Heidegger," p. 43.

29. Cf. *ibid.*, pp. 43-44.

30. Thomas Langan, *The Meaning of Heidegger* (New York: Columbia University Press, 1961), pp. 107-108.

31. Buber, *op. cit.*, p. 39.

32. Langan, *op. cit.*, p. 111.

33. Cf. *ibid.*

34. Robinson, "Hermeneutic since Barth," *op. cit.*, p. 48.

35. Martin Heidegger, *Holzweg* (Frankfurt: Vittario Klostermann, 1950), p. 110. Quoted by Langan, *op. cit.*, p. 110.

36. Cf. Langan, *op. cit.*, p. 115.

37. *Ibid.*, p. 111.

38. Cf. Langan, *op. cit.*, pp. 119ff. Cf. also my discussion of this aspect of Heidegger's thought in a review article of *The Later Heidegger and Theology* found in the *Christian Scholar*, XLVII (Spring, 1954), 73ff.

39. Cf. H. Paul Santmire, "I-Thou, I-It, and I-Ens," *Journal of Religion*, XLVIII, No. 3 (July, 1968), 260-273.

40. Cf. Langan, *op. cit.*, p. 114.

41. Cf. Sontag, *op. cit.*, p. 13.

42. Heidegger, *Was ist Metaphysik?* (Bonn: Verlag Fred. Cohen, 1930), p. 49. Quoted by Langan, *op. cit.*, p. 100.

43. Langan, *op. cit.*, p. 100. Cf. H. Ott, "Language and Understanding," *Union Seminary Quarterly Review*, XXI (March, 1966), 290-291.

44. Heidegger, *Holzweg*, pp. 301-302. Quoted by Langan, *op. cit.*, p. 146.

45. Robinson, "Hermeneutic since Barth," *op. cit.*, p. 48. For a highly critical review of Heidegger's concept of history see Moltmann, *op. cit.*, pp. 255ff.

46. Cf. Robinson, "The German Discussion of the Later Heidegger," pp. 74-75.

47. *The New Science*, par. 34.

48. Heinrich Ott, "The Historical Jesus and the Ontology of History," in *The Historical Jesus and the Kerygmatic Christ*, Carl E. Braaten and Roy A. Harrisville, eds. (Nashville: Abingdon Press, 1964), p. 160.

49. Ott, "The Historical Jesus and the Ontology of History," pp. 160-161.

50. Cf. Heinrich Zimmer, *Philosophies of India* (New York: Meridian, 1956), p. 548 *et passim.*

51. Ott, "The Historical Jesus and the Ontology of History," p. 161. Ott's italics.

52. *Ibid.,* p. 166.

53. Cf. Sontag, *op. cit.,* p. 13.

54. Ott, "The Historical Jesus and the Ontology of History," p. 157.

55. *Ibid.* Ott's italics.

56. *Ibid.*

57. Cf. Heinrich Ott, *Theology and Preaching,* trans. Harold Knight (London: Lutterworth Press, 1965), pp. 12-13.

58. Heinrich Ott, "What Is Systematic Theology?," in *The Later Heidegger and Theology,* James M. Robinson and John B. Cobb, Jr., eds. (New York: Harper & Row, 1963), p. 93.

59. Ott, *Denken und Sein,* p. 164. Quoted by Robinson, "The German Discussion of the Later Heidegger," p. 44.

60. Ott, "What Is Systematic Theology?" p. 84. Cf. Jürgen Moltmann, *op. cit.,* p. 244.

61. Cf. Ott, "The Historical Jesus and the Ontology of History," p. 145.

62. Ott, "What Is Systematic Theology?" p. 86.

63. Heinrich Ott, "Language and Understanding," *Union Seminary Quarterly Review,* XXI (March, 1966), 288.

64. Heinrich Ott, "Response to the American Discussion," in *The Later Heidegger and Theology,* p. 211.

65. *Ibid.,* p. 212.

66. Gerhard Ebeling, *The Nature of Faith,* trans. Ronald Gregor Smith (Philadelphia: Fortress Press, 1961), p. 187. Cf. p. 87.

67. Gerhard Ebeling, *Word and Faith,* trans. James W. Leitch (Philadelphia: Fortress Press, 1960), p. 318. Ebeling's italics.

68. Ebeling, *The Nature of Faith,* p. 182.

69. Ebeling, *Word and Faith,* p. 331.

70. Gerhard Ebeling, *God and Word,* trans. James W. Leitch (Philadelphia: Fortress Press, 1966), p. 19. Ebeling's italics.

71. *Ibid.,* p. 47.

72. Cf. *ibid.*

73. *Ibid.,* p. 47.

74. *Ibid.,* p. 48.

75. Cf. *ibid.,* p. 47.

76. Ebeling, *Word and Faith,* p. 323.

77. Buber, *I and Thou,* p. 39.

78. Ebeling, *Word and Faith,* p. 325. Cf. Ebeling, *God and Word,* Chap. I *et passim.*

79. Ebeling, *Word and Faith,* p. 325.

80. *Ibid.*, p. 428.
81. *Ibid.*
82. Ebeling, *The Nature of Faith*, p. 91.
83. *Ibid.*
84. Cf. *ibid.*
85. *Ibid.*, p. 92. Used with permission.
86. *Ibid.*, p. 90. Used with permission. Cf. Schubert Ogden, "What Sense Does It Make to Say, 'God Acts in History'?" *Journal of Religion*, XLIII (January, 1963), 7 *et passim.*
87. Ebeling, *Word and Faith*, p. 329.
88. Cf. James M. Robinson, "Kerygma and History in the New Testament," *The Bible in Modern Scholarship*, J. Philip Hyatt, ed. (Nashville: Abingdon Press, 1965), p. 119. Cf. Sontag, *op. cit.*
89. Ebeling, *Word and Faith*, p. 326.
90. Buber, *I and Thou*, p. 12.
91. Cf. Ebeling, *Word and Faith*, p. 331.
92. Cf. Ebeling, *The Nature of Faith*, p. 189.
93. Cf. Ebeling, *Word and Faith*, p. 331.
94. Cf. Robinson, "Hermeneutic since Barth," *op. cit.*, pp. 53-54.
95. Ernst Fuchs, *Hermeneutik* (Bad Canstatt: R. Mullerschon, 1958), p. 111. Quoted by Robinson, "Hermeneutic since Barth," p. 54. Cf. Buber's, "Man takes his stand in language and speaks from there."
96. Cf. Ernst Fuchs, "What Is a Language-event?" *Studies of the Historical Jesus*, trans. Andrew Scobie (Studies in Biblical Theology #42 [London: SCM, 1964]), p. 211.
97. *Ibid.*, p. 212. Fuchs's italics.
98. Ernst Fuchs, "The Essence of 'Language-event' and Christology," *Studies of the Historical Jesus*, p. 220.
99. Fuchs, "What Is a 'Language-event'?" p. 210.
100. Cf. Ebeling, *God and Word*, p. 41.
101. *Ibid.*
102. *Ibid.*
103. *Ibid.*, pp. 41-42.
104. Ebeling, *Word and Faith*, p. 328.
105. Ebeling, *The Nature of Faith*, p. 189. Used with permission. Cf. *Word and Faith*, p. 331.
106. Ernst Fuchs, "Language in the New Testament," *Studies of the Historical Jesus*, p. 77.
107. Ernst Fuchs, "The Essence of the 'Language-event' and Christology," *Studies of the Historical Jesus*, p. 220.
108. Ernst Fuchs, "Schluss der Vorlesung über das Johannesevangelium, Berlin S.S. 1968 (24.7.1958)," *Ergänzungscheft* to the *Hermeneutik*, p. 12. Quoted by Robinson, "Hermeneutic since Barth," pp. 52-53.

Chapter 5: THE FULLNESS OF REAL MUTUAL ACTION

1. Gordon D. Kaufman, "On the Meaning of 'God': Transcendence without Mythology," *New Theology No. 4,* Martin E. Marty and Dean G. Peerman, eds. (New York: Macmillan, 1967), pp. 69-98. Reprinted from the *Harvard Theological Review* (April, 1966).
2. Kaufman, *op. cit.,* p. 73. Used with permission.
3. *Ibid.,* p. 77.
4. *Ibid.,* p. 75. Kaufman's italics.
5. Cf. *ibid.,* pp. 76ff.
6. *Ibid.,* p. 80.
7. *Ibid.,* p. 84. Kaufman's italics.
8. *Ibid.*
9. *Ibid.,* p. 82. Kaufman's italics.
10. *Ibid.,* p. 82, n. 12. Kaufman's italics.
11. Cf. *ibid.,* pp. 82-83.
12. *Ibid.,* p. 81.
13. *Ibid.,* p. 85.
14. *Ibid.,* p. 87.
15. Cf. *ibid.,* p. 89.
16. *Ibid.* Used with permission.
17. *Ibid.,* p. 84.
18. Cf., e.g., Harvey, *op. cit.,* pp. 54ff.
19. Kaufman, *op. cit.,* p. 91.
20. *Ibid.,* pp. 91-92. Kaufman's italics. Used with permission.
21. *Ibid.,* p. 89.
22. *Ibid.,* p. 93.
23. *Ibid.,* p. 92. Kaufman's italics.
24. *Ibid.* Cf. p. 95.
25. Cf. *ibid.,* pp. 94ff.
26. *Ibid.,* p. 95. Used with permission. Since this portion of Kaufman's essay is not developed, the exposition of it which follows may contain some element of interpretation. I must, of course, accept responsibility for any inadequacy of interpretation.
27. *Ibid.*
28. Cf. *ibid.*
29. Cf. *ibid.*
30. *Ibid.,* p. 96.
31. *Ibid.,* pp. 97-98. Used with permission.
32. Fuchs, "What Is a 'Language-event'?" p. 210. Used with permission.
33. Ernst Fuchs, "Das Christusverständnis bei Paulus und im Johannesevangelium," *Marburger Theologische Studien,* H. Grass and W. G. Kümmel, eds. (Marburg: N. G. Elwert Verlag, 1963), Bd. 1, pp. 11-20. Used with permission. Quoted by Robinson, "Hermeneutic since Barth," pp. 60-61.

34. Robinson, "Hermeneutic since Barth," p. 61, n. 178.
35. Cf. Gordon Kaufman, "On the Meaning of 'Act of God,'"
Harvard Theological Review, 61 (1968), 196 *et passim*.
36. Cf. Ebeling, *The Nature of Faith*, Chap. XIII *et passim*.
37. Cf. Kaufman, "On the Meaning of 'Act of God,'" *passim*.
38. Ebeling, *Word and Faith*, p. 322.
39. *Ibid.*, p. 324.
40. Cf. Kaufman, "On the Meaning of 'God': Transcendence
without Mythology," p. 93, n. 25.
41. Cf. Schubert Ogden, "What Sense Does It Make to Say: 'God
Acts in History'?" *Journal of Religion*, XLIII (January, 1963), 16.
42. Gerhard Ebeling, *Evangelische Evangelienauslesung; Eine
Untersuchung zu Luthers Hermeneutik* (1942), pp. 382f. Quoted by
Robinson, "Hermeneutic since Barth," p. 64.
43. *Ibid.*
44. Vico, *The New Science*, par. 147.
45. Ernst Fuchs, "The New Testament and the Hermeneutical
Problem," *The New Hermeneutic*, p. 136. Fuchs's italics. Used with
permission.
46. Robinson, "Kerygma and History in the New Testament,"
op. cit., p. 119.
47. *Ibid.*, p. 120.

Chapter 6: PROSPECT FOR THE FUTURE

1. Justus George Lawler, "The Future of Belief Debate," *New
Theology No. 5*, Martin E. Marty and Dean G. Peerman, eds. (New
York: Macmillan, 1968), p. 183.
2. Quoted by Lawler, *op. cit.*, p. 183.
3. Cf. Leslie Dewart, *The Future of Belief* (New York: Herder
and Herder, 1966), esp. Chap. V.
4. *Ibid.*, p. 198. Since the death-of-God theology has gone out
of style with the same breathless rapidity with which it came in,
one hesitates even to write a note pertaining to it. Nevertheless, at
this point in Dewart's argument (and our own) the element of
truth and the principal contribution of the death-of-God theology
does come into view.
5. Dewart, *op. cit.*, p. 195.
6. Cf., *ibid.*, p. 177.
7. *Ibid.*, p. 200.
8. *Ibid.*, p. 177. Dewart's italics.
9. *Ibid.*, p. 177. Used with permission.
10. Cf., *ibid.*, p. 207.
11. There is, of course, substantial biblical warranty for this
position. The more obvious passages include Rom. 8:38-39; Col.
1:15ff; and the so-called nature miracles in the Gospels.
12. Dewart, *op. cit.*, p. 192. Dewart's italics. Used with permission.

13. See Theodosious Dobzhansky, "Evolution: Implications for Religion," *The Christian Century*, July 19, 1967, p. 938. It is true that Teilhard de Chardin's thought possesses a very limited recognition of the demonic or evil in nature; and this may well be one of its chief weaknesses.

14. Dewart, *op. cit.*, p. 210. Used with permission.

15. *Ibid.*, p. 211. Dewart's italics. Used with permission. Cf. the first phrase of this quotation with Vico's, "The true and the made are convertible."

16. Paul Tillich, *Theology of Culture*, ed. R. Kimball (New York: Oxford University Press, 1959), p. 42.

17. Dewart, *op. cit.*, p. 193. Dewart's italics.

18. Cf., *ibid.*, p. 195.

19. *Ibid.*, p. 197.

20. We would accept Dewart's statement about worship not only as one clarifying the modern perplexity about prayer better than do most books on the subject but also as one explaining succinctly how prayer is experienced from within the myth of history. Dewart writes: "Worship might be better understood as the rendering of ourselves present to the presence of God, whether in the interior prayer which sends no message to God but which receives his presence, or in the public and common ceremonies which visibly, audibly, and sensibly [and, by implication, historically] unite us through our collective presence to each other in the presence of the present God." *Ibid.*, p. 206. Used with permission.

21. Moltmann, *Theology of Hope*, pp. 49-50.

22. *Ibid.*, p. 50.

23. Cf. W. Richard Comstock, "Theology after the Death of God," *Cross-Currents*, XVI, No. 3 (Summer, 1966), 265-305.

24. Owen Barfield, *Saving the Appearances* (New York: Harcourt, Brace and World, n.d.), p. 167. Used with permission.

25. Quoted by Moltmann, *op. cit.*, p. 20.

26. Cf., *ibid.* This passage is an example of the many discussions in Moltmann's *Theology of Hope* in which the past, present, and future are held in balance. It is only in a limited number of polemical passages that the future is stressed unduly.

27. Cf., e.g., Martin E. Marty and Dean G. Peerman (eds.), *New Theology No. 5* (New York: Macmillan, 1968).

28. Moltmann, *op. cit.*, p. 22.

29. *Ibid.*

30. *Ibid.*

31. George A. Lindbeck, "The Framework of Catholic-Protestant Disagreement," in *The Word in History*, T. Patrick Burke, ed. (New York: Sheed and Ward, 1966), pp. 107-108. Italics added. © 1966 by the publisher. Used with permission.

32. Barfield, *op. cit.*, p. 170. Used with permission.

Index

Augustine, 10, 54
Autonomy, see History, autonomy of

Baillie, D. M., 61
Barfield, O., 2, 7n, 25, 156, 158n
Barr, J., 21
Barth, K., 25
Bergin, T. G., 34n, 38n, 41n, 59n
Berlin, I., 38n, 39n, 40n, 41ff., 47n, 51n, 55n, 59n
Bible, see History and Scripture
Bonhoeffer, D., 23n
Braaten, C., 68n
Brown, J., 39n
Buber, M., 5f., 27-30, 46, 51, 77, 95-98, 100, 102, 113, 116, 117n, 118n, 129, 138
Bultmann, R., 4, 37, 58f., 61, 66-93, 94, 120f., 144f.

Cahill, P. J., 67n, 84n, 85
Caponigri, A. R., 41n, 43n, 44n, 45f., 51, 52n, 55n, 67n
Cartesian philosophy, see History and Cartesian philosophy
Christ, and history, 4, 55, 88, 115, 154, 156ff.; pre-existence of, 56; two natures of, 56f., 82, 140-143; see Incarnation; Jesus
Christianity, distinctiveness of, 31f.; relation to Judaism, 22, 24f., 27f., 80; see History and ahistorical understanding
Church, 1ff., 18, 24, 26, 31-33, 47, 56, 61, 64f., 67, 83, 148
Civilization, see History and civilization
Cobb, J. B., 67n, 98n
Coleridge, S., 39

Collingwood, R. G., 13, 30n, 33n, 38, 55n, 59n, 82
Community, 1, 7, 55, 139, 146, 154n
Comstock, W. R., 156n
Content/form dichotomy, see History, subjectivity/objectivity in
Copleston, F., 40n
Covenant, 18-27, 51, 98
Creation, 7, 21-25, 27n, 105, 137, 139, 150
Croce, B., 55n
Culture, see History and civilization

Dasein, 99, 103ff.
"Death-of-God," 3f., 149, 149n
Decision, 70, 72, 75-80, 84, 88, 139, 144
Demythologization, 29, 47, 86-94, 108, 121ff.
Descartes, R., 5, 14, 33, 39-43, 47, 53, 98n, 103
Dewart, L., 2, 57, 149-154, 154n
Dobzhansky, T., 152n

Ebeling, G., 1, 57, 61n, 97, 107, 111-119, 120n, 138n, 139n, 142, 142n, 143n
Eichrodt, W., 19n, 23n, 24n
Eliot, T. S., 3
Eschatology, 7f., 79f., 85f., 104, 107, 118, 148, 152, 156
Essential thinking, see Originative thinking
Eucharist, see Sacraments and liturgy
Event, concept of, 22ff.; original relational, 6f., 27-32, 46, 51, 80, 105, 132-138, 147

175

Pre-understanding, 72ff., 117f.
Proclamation, 115-120
Promise and fulfillment, 1, 19f., 23, 34, 51f., 70, 127, 137, 148, 156f.
Protestantism, 78
Providence, 55

Reimarus, H., 58n
Revelation, 29, 64, 67, 79, 96, 153
Ricoeur, P., 71n, 92
Robinson, J. M., 61n, 65, 82, 97, 98n, 99, 100n, 101n, 105, 116, 118n, 136n, 146n

Sacraments and liturgy, 7, 92, 101f., 117, 119, 132, 150, 154, 154n
Salvation, 57
Sandmel, S., 60
Santmire, H. P., 102n
Scheler, M., 41n
Schniewind, J., 68n
Schweitzer, A., 60, 64ff.
Science, see History and natural science
Scripture, see History and Scripture
Secular, secularism, 3f., 21, 29f., 35f., 138f., 153
Sin, 26f., 27n, 29, 32, 55, 79, 84, 87
Sittler, J., 7n
Smart, J., 20n
Sontag, S., 45n, 94f., 103n, 108n, 116
Spengler, O., 11
Spirit, see God as Holy Spirit; Man, spirit of

Stevenson, W. T., 29n, 84n, 102n
Strauss, D. F., 60ff.

Teilhard de Chardin, P., 2, 7, 152n
Theology, theological situation, 7f., 30f., 33, 38, 48, 58, 139, 155f., 158
Theonomy, 152f.
Tillich, P., 50n, 153, 153n
Toynbee, A., 3, 10, 11
Transcendence, see God, transcendence and immanence of
Transparence (luminousness), 94f., 103, 107f., 111, 114, 121
Tuchman, B., 13, 15, 37

Van Buren, P., 3n, 35n
Verum et factum convertuntur, 41ff., 41n, 54, 132, 139, 147, 153n
Vichian philosophy, see History and Vichian philosophy
Vico, Giambattista, 2, 5, 10n, 15, 28, 32f., 36-57, 58f., 62, 65f., 68, 77, 95f., 98ff., 102, 105ff., 110, 113, 121, 132, 139, 141, 143, 145, 153n
Von Rad, G., 19n

Word, see God, word of; Man, word of
Wright, G., 24n

Yahweh, 19ff., 22ff., 28, 52
Yes-saying, 135, 142, 146

Zahrnt, H., 35n, 58n, 61n, 64, 65n
Zimmer, H., 108n